KEYNES AS A POLICY ADVISER

Other titles in this series

KEYNES: ASPECTS OF THE MAN AND HIS WORK (*edited by D. E. Moggridge*)
KEYNES AND INTERNATIONAL MONETARY RELATIONS (*edited by A. P. Thirlwall*)
KEYNES AND LAISSEZ-FAIRE (*edited by A. P. Thirlwall*)
KEYNES AND THE BLOOMSBURY GROUP (*edited by Derek Crabtree and A. P. Thirlwall*)

Keynes and Lloyd George at the Liberal Summer School, Cambridge, 1927

KEYNES AS A POLICY ADVISER

The Fifth Keynes Seminar held at the University of Kent at Canterbury 1980

edited by

A. P. THIRLWALL

Professor of Applied Economics
University of Kent at Canterbury

First published 1982 by
THE MACMILLAN PRESS LTD
London and Basingstoke
Companies and representatives
throughout the world

ISBN 0 333 32197 9

Photoset in Great Britain by
Redwood Burn Limited, Trowbridge, Wiltshire
and printed in Hong Kong

To the memory of Walter Hagenbuch
who helped so much with the Keynes seminars

Contents

List of Guests and Participants in Discussion

Sir Frederick Atkinson *Aldington, Kent*
Lord Balogh *London*
Professor A. J. Brown *University of Leeds*
Dr K. Burk *University of Oxford*
Professor W. Carr *University of Sheffield*
Sir Norman Chester *University of Oxford*
Professor A. W. Coats *University of Nottingham*
Mr Derek Crabtree *University of Kent*
Mr T. M. Farmiloe *London*
Professor W. Hagenbuch *University of Kent*
Rt Hon. Terence Higgins, PC, MP *London*
Sir Bryan Hopkin *University College, Cardiff*
Dr Susan Howson *Bank of England*
Lord Kahn *University of Cambridge*
Professor Lord Kaldor *University of Cambridge*
Dr Milo Keynes *Cambridge*
Mr Stephen Keynes *London*
Sir Henry Lintott *Cambridge*
Professor Donald E. Moggridge *University of Cambridge*
Mr R. G. Opie *University of Oxford*
Dr George Peden *University of Bristol*

Sir Austin Robinson *University of Cambridge*
Professor Joan Robinson *University of Cambridge*
Professor G. L. S. Shackle *Aldeburgh, Suffolk*
Professor H. Singer *University of Sussex*
Professor Robert Skidelsky *University of Warwick*
Dr Adrian Smith *University of Kent*
Dr D. Southern *University of Kent*
Professor A. P. Thirlwall *University of Kent*
Professor M. J. C. Vile *University of Kent*
Professor Tom Wilson *University of Glasgow*
Professor Donald Winch *University of Sussex*

Acknowledgements

The editor wishes to thank Dr Milo Keynes for the frontispiece, and Mrs Hilary Daly and Mrs Diana Guisinger in Keynes College for their help in transcribing the tapes of the seminar and for typing the final draft of the manuscript.

A. P. T.

Foreword

When the late Professor Spence first entertained the idea of a regular seminar to commemorate Lord Keynes, he was firmly convinced that in Keynes's life, thought and influence there lay more than ample material for a series of seminars. He was also a realist and aware of all the problems involved in organising such an event. It was always a distinct possibility that the first Keynes seminar would be the last!

It was, then, a particular pleasure to welcome people to the Fifth Keynes Seminar on 14 November 1980. An average of 400 students, academics and laymen were in attendance during the course of the afternoon. The theme of the seminar, 'Keynes as a Policy Adviser', had been suggested originally by Dr Milo Keynes, and found a ready response from the Keynes Seminar Organising Committee. Keynes took on the mantle of policy adviser, in both an official and an unofficial capacity, over a period of some thirty years, which culminated in his role as an architect of the Bretton Woods agreement in 1944 which laid the basis for the unprecedented prosperity of the world economy in the aftermath of war. In the inter-war period he had had the ready ear both of Prime Ministers and of Chancellors of the Exchequer, and rarely a day went by without a memorandum from his pen. In many ways, he is still advising us today. The oral evidence that he gave to the

Macmillan Committee in 1930 could be read with great profit now by those who are attempting to organise our economic affairs. The role of economic advisers in government itself is of more than topical interest, as the number of advisers has grown over the years against a background of declining economic performance.

From the distinguished guests who took part in our proceedings it will perhaps not be thought invidious to single out Lord Kahn, Professor Joan Robinson and Sir Austin Robinson as conveying a sense of continuity with Lord Keynes, and Dr Milo Keynes and Mr Stephen Keynes who provide a link with the family.

We are grateful to Mr Farmiloe and Macmillan for support and for continuing to publish the proceedings of the seminars, and also to the Vice-Chancellor, Dr Ingram, and the Faculty of Social Sciences of the University of Kent for financial assistance.

The burden of organisation of this and previous seminars was made lighter by the dedicated membership of Professor Walter Hagenbuch on the Seminar Committee, and his sudden death shortly after the seminar is a sore loss to the College. We shall miss his sage counsel and firm chairmanship at future seminars.

Keynes College
March 1981

Derek Crabtree
Master

Session 1

INTRODUCTION

Professor A. P. Thirlwall (Chairman)

Our first speaker this afternoon is Professor Lord Kaldor. Professor Kaldor needs no introduction to economists, but it is my pleasure to introduce him to this wider audience. Nicholas Kaldor came to England from Hungary in 1927 to study at the London School of Economics. Having imbibed the orthodox economics of the time, he was one of the first of the London School to be converted to Keynesianism, and from the mid-1930s was in close contact with Keynes. After spells in Europe and the United States after the war, he returned to England in 1949 to take up a Fellowship at King's College, Cambridge, and to join the Economics Faculty there. As a teacher, *provocateur*, Special Adviser to two Labour Chancellors of the Exchequer, and tax adviser to several developing countries, he has become something of a legendary figure (although, like all legends, the Kaldor legend has increasingly departed from the facts). His contribution to both theoretical and applied economics has been outstanding, as the papers in his eight volumes of collected writings testify. I invite him now to talk on 'Keynes as an Economic Adviser' with special reference to the period 1929–31 and Keynes's conversion to protection—which may have some contemporary relevance.

KEYNES AS AN ECONOMIC ADVISER[1]

Lord Kaldor

Keynes was an economic adviser, first and foremost; he was a theoretical economist and the creator of a new intellectual system second. *The General Theory of Employment, Interest and Money* is the foundation of modern macro-economics which I think will rank as the most important and the most distinct contribution which our century has added to the corpus of knowledge of socio-economic processes. Yet, after a study of Keynes's work as an adviser on current problems, I am convinced that the invention of the *General Theory* emerged as a by-product of his unceasing preoccupation with the most urgent issues of governmental (fiscal and monetary) policies.

There are two kinds of scientists in economics, as in other sciences. It would be wholly misleading to label them as the abstract theorists and the empiricists, although this is how they are often distinguished. There is one type of thinker whose main interest is in pure *deduction*—in exploring the full implications of certain basic postulates. The other type starts from a concrete problem and wishes to explore it as such, and in the course of exploration forges his own tools, and may be led, step by step, to extend the scope of his enquiry so as to cover a wider range of phenomena. Walras is perhaps the most distinguished example of an economist who wished to explore the laws of operation of a market economy from certain basic, a priori postulates concerning competition, the nature of wants, and resources, without testing his results at any stage in the light of empirical knowledge. Keynes is an economist who, until relatively late in life, never really questioned the intellectual system of economics which he inherited—or the political principles derived from it—but who was intensely interested in how the performance of particular institutions could be improved, and from an early stage thought about economic problems 'in the concrete', so to speak; he could not conceptualise the phenomena observed in abstraction from their measurement. So he maintained in all his thinking a close liaison between induction and deduction—in much the same way as modern scientists who are ready to seek a solution to a concrete problem without aiming at a comprehensive explanation. Thus physicists, engaged on operational research during the last war, applied their intellectual abilities to particular hypotheses derived from observation. This can be done without reference to general principles; but for a scientist it is essential that his particular findings should be consistent with accepted principles, and that he should be ready to tackle the latter if some basic inconsistency is discovered.

Keynes belonged to the latter category. As an economist and a pupil of Marshall, he was remarkably conformist in his acceptance of established theory, without questioning its fundamentals—until such a questioning was forced on him by the need to find consistency between the established views and his own intuitive hypotheses. Even so, he never succeeded in cutting himself loose entirely—as he said at the end of the Preface to the *General Theory*: 'the difficulty lies not in new ideas but in escaping from old ones, which ramify, for those brought up as most of us have been, into every corner of our minds'.

Keynes's activities as an economic adviser began before the First World War and ended with his death one year after the end of hostilities in Europe in the

Second World War. I shall not be concerned today with his work for the Treasury in either of the two world wars, but only with his activities as a policy adviser in the 1920s and particularly in the early part of the 1930s. Throughout this period his views and ideas were in a continuing state of evolution, with frequent changes forced upon him by his close observation of fast-moving policies and events.

Thus in the early 1920s we find him a passionate liberal and a passionate defender of free trade. Speaking in Manchester in October 1922, he said that

> every scrap of experience which accumulates emphasises the blindness and disastrous folly [of any form of protection.] Formerly free trade was a desirable end to increased wealth. It has now become a necessary and essential defence against a crushing poverty. Unless we direct our resources into the directions where they are most productive, we shall not be able to gain a living at all.
>
> My financial policy for Liberalism is therefore ... uncompromising Free Trade.[2]

He attacked Baldwin's advocacy of protection in two articles in *The Nation and Athenaeum*, 24 November and 1 December 1923:

> a tariff will not remedy any of the main causes of unemployment. Why does Mr. Baldwin think that it will? I believe ... that this is because he is a victim of the protectionist fallacy in its crudest form. If we keep out an imported article, he argues, which it is not impossible to make at home, some Englishman, now unemployed, will be employed on making it. *Voila tout*—Mr. Baldwin sees no further than that.

> Does he suppose that we now get that import for nothing? If it has crossed his mind that we probably pay for it by an export, is it his idea that for the future we should make a present of that export to the foreigner? I have found no indication that Mr. Baldwin and his friends have advanced a step beyond this elementary folly when they prescribe a tariff to cure unemployment.[3]

In addition to having an uncompromising attitude to free trade with no exceptions he was for: drastic economies in public expenditure; no reduction in taxation until the budget has been balanced, including provision for sinking funds; no more expensive projects in the fields of health or education, although existing social expenditure should be preserved; and he thought that only a Liberal Government could be relied upon to adhere to such policies.

In 1924 we find him worried over the persistence of unemployment which he attributes to 'an attempt on the part of organised labour, or the community as a whole, to maintain real wages at a higher level than the underlying economic conditions are able to support', given the deteriorating terms of trade between manufactures and primary products, resulting from population pressures.

And with regard to the stability of the price level, he accepts the Marshallian version of the quantity theory of money, with the amendment that k in the Cambridge quantity equation is not stable but is capable of sharp fluctuations, so that in order to keep the price level steady, the quantity of money needs to be varied in a contrary direction, so as to counterbalance changes in k.

His advocacy of a system of 'managed' exchange

rates (in place of a return to the gold standard) in the *Tract on Monetary Reform* was in the interest of securing stability of the internal price level through variation in the exchange rate relative to gold—for the same kind of reasons for which German economists advocated a 'floating rate' in the 1960s so as to avoid 'importing inflation' from the United States. By present-day standards this was a thoroughly 'monetarist' position.

And there was no more than a foretaste of his future views in certain passages of the *Tract* which compare the disadvantages of deflation with those of inflation and explain why the former is likely to be more disastrous in its consequences than the latter. Still he believed that under a policy of a floating exchange rate, appropriate monetary policies could secure stable prices and allow the pound to appreciate as world-prices (or gold prices) rise *relatively* to United Kingdom prices—until the point is reached where we could return to the gold standard in the manner of Sweden, which allowed its currency to float *above* gold parity but not to fall *below* it.

However, by the time Britain returned to the gold standard at pre-war parity in 1925, Keynes was a wholehearted opponent, summarising his views in a pamphlet entitled *The Economic Consequences of Mr Churchill*.[4] This spelled out the effects on foreign trade and on employment of the over-valuation of the pound, which he put at 10 per cent. This pamphlet spells out much more clearly than he had done before that over-valuation necessitates a downward adjustment of wages to be brought about by credit restrictions, and the *modus operandi* of credit restriction is '*the deliberate intensification of unemployment*' [italics as in the original].[5]

This is the earliest paper of Keynes which could have been written today, and which would be just as powerful as a criticism of the current policies of Mrs Thatcher as those of Stanley Baldwin in 1925. Monetary policy, as Keynes makes clear in that pamphlet, the basis of the agitation for the necessity to cut wages in the coal industry and elsewhere, is 'simply a campaign against the standard of life of the working classes'. It is worth quoting from the concluding sentence:

> our present policy of deliberately intensifying unemployment by keeping a tight hold on credit, just when on other grounds it ought to be relaxed, so as to force adjustments by using the weapon of economic necessity against individuals and against particular industries, is a policy which the country would never permit if it knew what was being done.

One cannot read this pamphlet of July 1925 without feeling that here is a mind with an extraordinary sense of intuition, which would be capable of grasping the important consequences of policies without the aid of a systematic framework which was still very far from being built.

The *Treatise on Money*, written in the course of the next few years, was intended to provide the systematic framework underlying the views or assertions made in the pamphlet. In certain aspects it represented a breakthrough in introducing the distinction between savings and investment and in showing that the level of profits will be so varied that *ex post* these differences disappear through abnormally high and low profits resulting from high or low investment relative to savings.

But it was too much concerned with money and with movements in the price-level; the notion of how windfall profits arise is part of his theory of changes in the *price-level*. We look in vain for any elaboration of the bold assertion of the Churchill pamphlet that credit restrictions operate *through* the deliberate intensification of unemployment. There is hardly any reference to employment and unemployment; there is no analysis of the link between price-level changes, whether or not caused by monetary factors, and their consequences upon the real economy.

However, the writing of his book must have provided a tremendous stimulus to the rapid development of his own ideas as regards the major macro-economic relationships operating on the level of output and employment, as distinct from prices. For in the very same year in which the *Treatise on Money* was published, indeed some six months earlier, Keynes gave detailed oral evidence to the newly appointed Macmillan Committee of which he was a member, which took up five sessions and lasted 16 hours.[6] This has not hitherto been available, as Keynes, being a member of the Committee, gave the systematic exposition of his views in private sessions. It was a masterly effort which was much superior to the elaborate abstractions of the 'pure theory' of the *Treatise* and which put forward a macro-economic 'model' of the British economy which in certain respects was superior also to that put forward six years later in the *General Theory*. This is because his analysis specifically referred to Britain and examines the *modus operandi* of the British economy in the context of her peculiar institutions. Exports, the trade balance, the flow of overseas lending, the nature of the adjustment mechanism in foreign trade, the instruments employed by the Bank of England, are brought into relationship with one another to show how the system generates a low employment trap, as a result of the high interest rates enforced by the Bank of England which are made necessary by the need to limit overseas lending to the amount that the level of net exports (the current account balance) permits. High interest rates are necessary to hold down overseas investment; but they *also* hold down home investment, with the result that the sum of the two is well below the level required to offset full employment savings. Hence the chronic unemployment problem. He also makes a sharp distinction between profits and other types of incomes generated by productive activity. High profits are the consequence of high investment, investment may be 'financed' by money borrowed from the banking system, but the profits arising as a result of (income-generating) investment activity enable the loan to be repaid so that the new assets become the property of the entrepreneur *gratis*, so to speak, as they are paid for out of the profits which the investment activity itself generates.

He diagnoses the fundamental trouble of the British economy as arising from the over-valuation of the pound, aggravated since 1925 on account of the fall in world prices, which is responsible for the constraints generated by insufficient exports. That, combined with London's role as the world's financial centre, requires the restrictionist credit policy which deliberately 'intensifies unemployment'.

He then considers systematically all the possible ways in which the situation could be remedied. He is against going off gold, or of changing the gold parity of sterling, both of which would 'impair London's role as a world financial centre' (though curiously the benefits derived by the country from this role are never discussed). He considers a general reduction of money wages as something that can be ruled out, because resistance to cuts in money wages has existed for centuries, and not just as the result of trade unions whose role in the situation, he argues, is much exaggerated. This leaves the stimulus to home investment through government subsidies or some system of divorcing the interest rates charged on foreign loans from those charged to domestic borrowers. Finally, he considers a 'revenue tariff', charged at a flat rate on all imports with a corresponding bounty on all exports. The difficulties with the separation of interest rates to home and foreign borrowers lead him to regard the tariff-cum-bounty proposal *faute de mieux* as the best solution. The majority of the Committee were willing to go along with this. Only two members, Professor Gregory and Lord Bradbury, rejected the idea, though the former signed the report, subject to a lengthy reservation.

In his oral evidence to the Macmillan Committee, Keynes goes into considerable detail as to the reasons for his conversion to protection. Keynes saw the fallacy of the free trade doctrine if the system gets 'jammed at the point of unemployment'—as he put it. In such circumstances, several of the free trade arguments become, in part, arguments for protection. In fact, he claimed, the free trade argument for simultaneous internal and external equilibrium is very similar to the Bank Rate policy which he rejected. For example, he says, suppose the McKenna duties are taken off. The balance of payments would deteriorate; there would be a loss of gold; this would lead to an increase in the Bank Rate, to higher unemployment and depressed wages, which in theory should lead to a readjustment of labour and a restoration of equilibrium. The trouble is the system does not work so fluidly and 'the alternative for a time may be producing motor cars (under protection) or producing nothing'. Even McKenna, who described himself to the Committee as a lifelong free trader, admitted that 'the only condition in which I can foresee any rational agreement throughout the world to get back to something like Free Trade is if we protect'. Keynes went on:

> The virtue of free trade is that it does bring money

> wages down and it does not bring real wages down, whereas protection is not so likely to bring down money wages, it is much more likely to bring down real wages. But the virtue of protection is that it does the trick, whereas in present conditions free trade does not. Therefore the question is, how far one is prepared to be governed by short-run considerations, and it seems to me, when one has by virtue of Mr. McKenna got some duties, it would be a very strange act to aggravate the position by removing them. When it is a question of putting on new duties it is a much more difficult question, and it also depends on what alternative remedies there are and how long the present situation is to last. If we are jammed for some time I think we should get some immediate relief by well adjusted tariffs.[7]

He conceded that once tariffs are imposed it may be difficult to get them off again. The question is how much is one willing to pay for an immediate benefit.

Keynes then links up the argument for protection with his earlier theoretical analysis of the imbalance in the economy between saving and investment, which he recognised as the source of the difficulty.

> Protection is another way of increasing the amount of our foreign investment and that is how it profoundly works in with my argument. The other way is by increasing our exports. We can increase our favourable foreign balance on income account by diminishing our imports, and the real contribution that protection makes is that, by diminishing our imports, it increases the amount of our foreign investment and brings exactly the same sort of relief as the first four remedies I was discussing [viz. gold revaluation; money wage reductions; export

> bounties and increased efficiency]. . . . If it is essential for equilibrium that we should invest abroad on a larger scale than at present, the protectionist way of doing it may be the method of least resistance, because it does not require reduction of money wages and it has less effect . . . in turning the terms of trade against us. . . . It may be that the free trade method of increasing our foreign investment has broken down; if so, there may be something to be said for the protectionist method of attaining the same result . . . free trade . . . assumes that if you throw men out of work in one direction you re-employ them in another. As soon as that link in the chain is broken the whole of the free trade argument breaks down.[8]

He also stressed the aspect of business confidence; that protection would revive optimistic expectations: 'That is a psychological argument; it is making a concession to meet a temporary situation. I regard it as drug taking.'

There can be no doubt, however, that he was a reluctant protectionist, and that, indeed, he vacillated. Having stated the case for protection, he says at the next meeting of the Committee on the 6 March 1930:

> I have not reached a clear cut opinion as to where the balance of advantage lies, I am frightfully afraid of protection as a long-term policy; I am sure it is radically unsound, if you take a long enough view, but we cannot always afford to take long views, and I am also equally clear that there are certain short-term advantages in protection.

He claimed that one factor causing him vacillation was that 'it is extremely difficult for anyone of free trade origin . . . to speak in a way that he himself believes to be quite truthful and candid without laying himself open to misrepresentation.... It is very difficult, I think, to be quite candid and at the same time not to give a false impression.'[9]

Much the same issues were thrashed out in the autumn of the same year by the Committee of Economists of the Economic Advisory Council. In the middle of 1930, the Prime Minister, Ramsay MacDonald, sent a series of questions to the members of the Economic Advisory Council pertaining to the current economic situation. Keynes replied on 10 July suggesting the setting up of a small committee of professional economists to consider at least the first question: What in your view are the chief causes of our present industrial position? Keynes suggested the membership of the committee and in the meantime gave his own brief answers to the questions posed, which included the consideration of protection. He claimed four advantages: it is the quickest and easiest way to improve the foreign balance; the free trade argument is premised on full employment equilibrium; a tariff will yield budget revenue; and protection will turn the terms of trade in Britain's favour. He declared 'I am no longer a free-trader ... in the old sense of the term to the extent of believing in a very high degree of national specialisation and abandoning any industry which is unable for the time being to hold its own. Where wages are immobile, this would be an extraordinarily dangerous doctrine to follow'.[10] Keynes maintained that in this sense there are no free traders left!

The Committee of Economists included, in addition to Keynes as Chairman, Pigou, Josiah Stamp, H. D. Henderson and Lionel Robbins. Keynes succeeded in producing an agreed report which is, moreover, a coherent document despite the fact that it incorporates sections written by members of different persuasions.

Keynes was clearly far ahead of the others in understanding the role of investment and exports, even though the basic tool of the *General Theory*, the multiplier, invented by R. F. Kahn in the following year, did not make its appearance in Keynes's expositions until two years later. Pigou and Robbins both hankered after money wage reduction as the best remedy (as Gregory did in his Addendum to the Macmillan report) and Robbins (very much younger than the others) was so horrified at the very mention of protection in any shape or form that he refused to sign the report and insisted on submitting a separate report of his own.

The fact that a report could be agreed on by the majority of the Committee was a great triumph for Keynes's powers of persuasion and his willingness to compromise for the sake of agreement (he incorporated long sections of Robbin's exposition of the causes of the slump in his own draft which remained despite the fact that Robbins did not sign the Report). The Report was signed on 24 October, four days before Parliament reassembled on 28 October.

The Report gives prominence to a reduction of money wages which was the remedy most generally favoured by economists of the period and the only remedy which was considered 'uncontroversial'. However, Keynes managed to incorporate in the Report a section spelling out the inherent difficulties in pursuing this policy and the unsettling effect on society of depressing wages in some industries and not in others. A section on wage-subsidies was added (presumably on Pigou's initiative) though not seriously pursued. The idea of devaluation was briefly mentioned and then dismissed—'none of us are prepared to recommend it at the present time'. However, tariffs were favoured by three members, Keynes, Henderson and Stamp, while Keynes and Stamp alone favoured

Keynes's 'tariff-cum-bounty' proposal which was put forward as the equivalent of a devaluation on trade account.

The Report was not well received by the Cabinet who took the view that while the Report was 'prolific in suggestions of a general character it contained no practical propositions to which immediate effect could be given'.[11]

Meanwhile the world economic crisis intensified. In the Cabinet, Snowden represented the view that the only way to cope with the crisis was by retrenchment. The government set up a Committee on National Expenditure (the May Committee) in February—on the insistence of the Liberals as well as the Conservative Opposition—which reported in August and recommended a 20 per cent cut in unemployment benefits. The Cabinet Committee considering the Report then reduced this to 10 per cent, but even this was not acceptable to the full Cabinet; so, under pressure from the New York bankers—who *insisted* that salary cuts alone were not enough in the absence of a cut in unemployment benefit—MacDonald tendered the resignation of his government, and a National Government was formed on a comprehensive programme of cuts, introduced in a second Budget in September. This contained expenditure cuts of £70 million and tax increases of £90 million, as well as a provision prohibiting further borrowing by the unemployment fund and further cutbacks in local authority and capital expenditures.

On reading about these events one has the peculiar feeling 'we've been here before', until one realises that one's memory played a trick—the resemblance is to events that are happening *now* and not to events in the yet more distant past.

The Budget was presented on 10 September and on 16 September Keynes told an all-party group of MPs in the House of Commons that the 'Government's programme is one of the most wrong and foolish things which Parliament has deliberately perpetrated in my lifetime'.

Earlier, Keynes came out openly in favour of a revenue tariff in an article in the *New Statesman*, 7 March—a popular version of which appeared in the *Daily Mail* six days later under the title of 'A Plea to Lifelong Free Traders'—advocating a 15 per cent imposition on all manufactures and semi-manufactures and 5 per cent on food.

Keynes declared:

> Free traders may, consistently with their faith, regard a revenue tariff as our iron ration, which can be used only in emergency. The emergency has arrived. Under cover of the breathing space and the margin of financial strength thus afforded us, we could frame a policy and a plan, both domestic and international, for marching to the assault against the spirit of contractionism and fear.
>
> If, on the other hand, free traders reject these counsels of expediency, the certain result will be to break the present government and to substitute for it, in the confusion of a crisis of confidence, a Cabinet pledged to a full protectionist programme. I am not unaccustomed to being in a minority. But on this occasion I believe that 90 per cent of my countrymen will agree with me.[12]

The article set the cat among the pigeons, leading to a virulent controversy with Beveridge, Robbins, Gregory and numerous others. Lionel Robbins accused Keynes of abandoning 'the service of high and worthy ideals in international relations for the service of the mean and petty devices of economic nationalism'.[13]

Keynes replied that:

> it is a poor retort, perhaps, to this, to say that one must not let one's sense of the past grow stronger than one's sense of the present and of the future, or sacrifice the substance for the symbol. But I can at least say that my practical aims are to avoid a disastrous process of competitive international wage cutting, and the social strife which this would bring; to enable this country to resume the financial leadership of the world which we alone are capable of using in the general interest; and to prevent a domestic political reaction which might delay progress towards international peace and interrupt our policy in India.[14]

Keynes then wrote a series of three short articles in the *New Statesman*, which re-read, show him to be the intellectual master—greatly superior to all his critics. In one of the pieces he registers a mild complaint against what he calls the undercurrent of moral reprobation which he detects in some quarters: 'I seem to see the elder parrots sitting round and saying "You can rely upon us". Every day for 30 years, regardless of the weather, we have said "What a lovely morning!" But this is a bad bird. He says one thing one day and something else the next.'[15]

Some of this controversy—with Cyril Asquith and William Beveridge—was carried on in the letter columns of *The Times*—in that of 1 April 1931, for example, which answered Beveridge by a *reductio ad absurdum*. Beveridge's position was that, while a reduction in imports does not help employment because it causes an equivalent reduction in exports, an increase in imports would be bad because it would not cause a corresponding increase in exports!

Many of Keynes's critics questioned his arithmetic concerning the *yield* of a revenue tariff, arguing that the tariff is likely to reduce imports by some £70 million or more and the net yield of the duty would not be more than £40 million, instead of £50 million. Keynes pointed out that the greater the import-reducing effect of the tariff the greater would be the substitution of home-produced goods for imports, and the greater the saving on the dole and the extra revenue from income tax, etc., due to higher domestic incomes and employment.[16]

Up to a few years ago, I would have said that the 'Keynesian revolution' made it impossible to advance the jejune arguments against import controls which Keynes's critics deployed in the spring of 1931. But now I am not so sure. The rapid decline of learning and intelligence as revealed, for example, by the quality of the arguments employed by members of the present government, makes one doubt whether there has been any lasting progress in understanding in the last fifty years.

In a letter to an American friend, Walter Case, of 14 September 1931, Keynes wrote:

> To read the newspapers just now is to see bedlam let loose. Every person in the country of super asinine properties, everyone who hates social progress and loves deflation, feels that his hour has come, and frequently announces how, by refraining from every form of economic activity, we can all become very prosperous again.

The Budget, though it reduced the Public Sector Borrowing Requirement (PSBR) of those days by some £180 million (in a full year) or 4.5 per cent of the GNP at current prices,[17] did not suffice to stem the drain on the reserves, so that in just over a week, on Friday, 18 September, the decision had to be made to suspend the gold convertibility of the pound; the necessary legislation was introduced and passed on Monday 21 September. Keynes foresaw it coming as shown by his letter to the Prime Minister of 5 August, in which he said that 'it is now too late to avoid this' and urged that if it were done immediately 'disaster could be converted into success' and we could win hegemony for a new currency union which most Empire countries would join and at some stage countries of South America, Asia, Central Europe, Italy and Spain as well. But it was not to be. The Bank, supported by the government, sought loans in Paris and New York to save the pound and accepted the conditions of a deflationary programme in return. The deflationary programme was quickly introduced and adopted but it failed to save the pound.

Keynes's reaction was one of immense relief. In an article in the *Sunday Express* of 27 September, far from gloating 'I told you so', or 'we could have done it much earlier without all this borrowing, the imposition of a highly deflationary Budget and the unnecessary loss of gold', he felt proud that by defending the pound to the last breath the 'claims of honour have been, in the judgment of the whole world, satisfied to the utmost' and so 'out of the ashes the City of London will rise again with undiminished honour. For she has played the game up to the limits of quixotry even at the risk of driving British trade almost to a standstill.'

In a letter to *The Times* written on the following day (28 September) he emphasises that the abandonment of the gold standard removes the need for a general tariff, and

> it is impossible to have a rational discussion about tariffs so long as the currency question is altogether unsolved. . . . And it is the latter which is urgent and important. . . . It is at present a non-party issue. . . . It offers immense opportunities for leadership by this country. We are probably in a position to carry the whole of the Empire and more than half of the rest of the world with us, and thus rebuild the financial supremacy of London on a firm basis.[18]

He was, therefore, much opposed to a general election which, as could be foreseen, would mean the return of a new Parliament with a clear majority of Conservatives who were committed to protection.

And so it occurred. The new government which came in after the October election with Neville Chamberlain as Chancellor of the Exchequer, proceeded to introduce a general tariff on imports of manufactures as quickly as possible. Since the government contained several ministers who were totally opposed to protection in all forms, a new precedent was created by abrogating the principle of collective Cabinet responsibility for this occasion and four ministers (Samuel, Snowden, Sinclair and Maclean) were permitted to register their dissent and to speak against the Bill in Parliament. Chamberlain followed Keynes's plan for a flat-rate tariff of 10 per cent (at the time when Keynes was no longer in favour of this) together with the creation of an Import Duties Advisory Committee to recommend higher duties on some or all products.[19]

Soon Keynes was slowly moving towards protection again, however, as is shown by the two articles on 'national self-sufficiency' published in the *New Statesman* in July 1933. He wrote:

> I sympathise, therefore, with those who would mini-

> mise, rather than those who would maximise, economic entanglement between nations. Ideas, knowledge, art, hospitality, travel—these are things which should of their nature be international. But let goods be homespun whenever it is reasonably and conveniently possible; and, above all, let finance be primarily national. Yet, at the same time, those who seek to disembarrass a country of its entanglements should be very slow and wary. It should not be a matter of tearing up roots, but of slowly training a plant to grow in a different direction.[20]

However, the arguments advanced in favour of greater self-sufficiency were based on the desirability of reduced dependence on the outside world; they did not touch the far more vital issue of how import controls could secure higher levels of employment and higher rates of economic growth than could be had under free trade. Though Keynes was aware of the theory of the foreign trade multiplier, just then put forward by Harrod,[21] he did not think out its full implications as he no doubt would have done had he lived through the British economy of the post-war period, and observed the effects of the adoption of policies of trade liberalisation, and the formation of customs unions in the 1960s and 1970s.

As it was, the abandonment of the gold standard and the adoption of a high level of import duties on manufactured goods ushered in the fastest period of economic growth in British history—but without anyone becoming fully aware of this fact while it happened. As we now know, in the years 1933–7 manufacturing output increased by 8 per cent a year, manufacturing employment by 4.1 per cent a year and productivity by 3.9 per cent a year. In 1937 output exceeded that of 1932 by 50 per cent and the previous peak of 1929 by

33.5 per cent. As against that, the 1929 peak output of manufacturing was only 11 per cent above that of the 1925 peak and only 12 per cent above 1913. Steel production increased from 5 million tons in 1932 to 13 million tons in 1937. GDP as a whole increased by 20.6 per cent in five years (or 3.8 per cent a year) whereas the *whole* increase in national real output between 1913 and 1937 was only 23.3 per cent, 86 per cent of which was telescoped into the four years 1933–7. Indeed the United Kingdom was the only country in the world which exceeded its pre-Depression national peak output of 1929. Germany had only just reached it while all the others remained well below it.[22]

When the National Government came into office, the Economic Advisory Council was put on ice and the Committee of Economists was replaced by the Committee on Economic Information chaired by Stamp, with Keynes, Citrine, Cole, Lewis Salter and Simon as members, and H. D. Henderson as Secretary. They were later joined by two Treasury officials, Sir Frederick Leith-Ross (Chief Economic Adviser to the government) and Sir Frederick Phillips. This Committee issued a series of remarkable reports and was instrumental in changing the 'prevailing view' of the Treasury away from the orthodoxy of the 1920s and towards active anti-cyclical demand management based on the cheap money policy and also on fiscal policies, on the lines of the later war-time White Paper on Full Employment.

One of its earliest proposals was the so-called Keynes–Henderson plan for an international note issue, put forward in the Committee's fourth report of July 1932, and intended for the coming World Economic Conference. This plan, which was never put forward for adoption by the government (mainly, it appears, owing to lack of United States support), is reproduced in some detail in Keynes's pamphlet *The Means to Prosperity* of March 1933.[23]

This paper is remarkable for the many changes in Keynes's views after the abandonment of the gold standard in 1931. It contains two themes: the first concerns internal expansion through State-financed loan expenditure on housing and public works, and is remarkable for its detailed exposition of the theory of the (home-investment) multiplier; the second contains far-reaching proposals for the restoration of world prosperity by means of increasing world demand through increased loan-expenditure all round. For this purpose Keynes proposed that a World Economic Conference be called with a view to establishing an international note-issuing institution which would provide every member country with gold notes that they were pledged to accept in lieu of payment in the same way as gold, and which would be issued to each country up to a maximum quota (determined by their 1928 gold reserve)[24] in exchange for National Gold Bonds.

Keynes assumed (both here and later, in the plans leading to Bretton Woods) that the mere provision of additional liquidity would prove sufficient to get the wheels of prosperity moving as it would be certain to be followed by an increase in the purchases of member countries from other countries. He was anxious to stress, if I may adapt an old adage, that now that Britain had saved herself by her exertions she could save others by her example. He was horrified by the mushroom growth of restrictive currency and trade measures which followed upon the events of 1931 and was anxious that 'unsound international practices which have become common under the stress of hard circumstances such as exchange restrictions, the immobilisation of foreign balances, tariffs and quotas which are not in pursuance of permanent national policies' should be brought to an end and the money markets of the 'stronger financial centres be re-opened'. He recommended that participation in the currency scheme be withheld 'from any country which was acting in defiance of its international agreements and obligations'. And he concludes:

> There remains, however, one essential condition upon which I have not yet touched. The notes would be gold notes and the participants would agree to accept them as the equivalent of gold. This implies that the national currencies of each participant would stand in some defined relationship to gold. *It involves, that is to say, a qualified return to the gold standard.*[25]
>
> It may seem odd that I, who have lately described gold as a 'barbaric relic' should be discovered as an advocate of such a policy, at the time when the orthodox authorities of this country are laying down conditions for our return to gold which they must know are incapable of fulfilment ... [but] I believe that gold has received such a gruelling that conditions might now be laid down for its further management which would not have been acceptable otherwise.

And what were these conditions? They are not much different from those found in the Articles of Association of the International Monetary Fund, complemented by those which animated the Havana Charter and GATT. After a nightmare interlude, the English liberal internationalism (or shall I say evangelism), driven by the sentiments which inspired the *Economic Consequences of the Peace*, re-asserted its dominion.

In conclusion, it may not be out of place to quote two brief passages from the autobiography of Bertrand

Russell:

> Keynes's intellect was the sharpest and clearest that I have ever known. When I argued with him I felt that I took my life in my hands, and I seldom emerged without feeling something of a fool. I was sometimes inclined to feel that so much cleverness must be incompatible with depth, but I do not think this feeling was justified.

And the other:

> He was always inclined to overwork, in fact it was overwork that caused his death. Once in the year 1904, when I was living in an isolated cottage in a vast moor without roads, he wrote and asked if I could promise him a restful weekend. I replied confidently in the affirmative, and he came. Within five minutes of his arrival the Vice-Chancellor turned up full of University business. Other people came unexpectedly to every meal, including six to Sunday breakfast. By Monday morning we had had twenty-six unexpected guests and Keynes, I fear, went away more tired than he came. On Sunday, August 2nd, 1914, I met him hurrying across the Great Court of Trinity. I asked him what the hurry was and he said he wanted to borrow his brother-in-law's motorcycle to go to London. 'Why don't you go by train?', I said. 'Because there isn't time', he replied. I did not know what his business might be, but within a few days the bank rate, which panic-mongers had put up to ten per cent, was reduced to five per cent. This was his doing.[26]

NOTES

1. In preparing the paper the author is grateful to Professor Donald Moggridge for providing access to the proofs of volumes XIX and XX of *The Collected Writings of John Maynard Keynes* (published by Macmillan Press, on behalf of the Royal Economic Society), entitled *Activities 1922–29: The Return to Gold and Industrial Policy*, and *Activities 1929–31: Rethinking Employment and Unemployment Policies*.
2. *Collected Writings*, vol. XIX, pp. 3, 4.
3. Ibid., p. 154.
4. He could not have suspected that Churchill himself was a strong opponent though he deferred, as Chancellor of the Exchequer, to the unanimous advice he received from the Treasury and the Bank of England.
5. *Collected Writings*, vol. IX, p. 218.
6. See *Collected Writings*, vol. XX, pp. 38–157.
7. Ibid., p. 115.
8. Ibid., p. 117.
9. Ibid., p. 120.
10. Ibid., pp. 379–80.
11. Minutes of a Cabinet Committee on Trade Policy, chaired by Snowden.
12. *Collected Writings*, vol. IX, p. 238.
13. *Collected Writings*, vol. XX, p. 497.
14. Ibid., p. 497.
15. Ibid., p. 502.
16. Letter to the *New Statesman*, 16 March 1931. It is a pity he did not carry his thoughts further on this matter. He would have reached the conclusion that for any given level of exports there is an optimal tariff which secures the volume of imports consistent with full employment.
17. In other words, it was the equivalent of a reduction by £8.5 billion expressed in present-day prices and incomes, or about three times as much as Mrs Thatcher has been aiming for in November 1980.
18. *The Times*, 29 September 1931.
19. This Committee soon recommended that the general rate of the tariff be increased to 20 per cent, with a special 33.5 per cent on steel and chemicals. (Motor cars and some other products were already subject to a 33.5 per cent import duty under the McKenna legislation.)
20. *Collected Writings*, vol. XX, ch. 3.
21. *International Economics* (Cambridge: Cambridge Economic Handbooks, 1933).
22. Rearmament did not play any important role in industrial production until 1938 and after. However, the building boom induced by a fall in interest rates was an important contributory factor. Apart from this (which clearly cannot account for the very rapid growth of production right across the industrial field, and particularly in the 'new' industries of electrical engineering, motors and cycles, chemicals, etc., the great bulk of the output of which was absorbed in the home market) the protection afforded both by exchange

depreciation and the introduction of across-the-board import duties for manufacturers, must have been the main factors responsible. Existing studies, chiefly by H. W. Richardson, play down the importance of the new tariffs but his statistical findings depend on a comparison of the censuses of 1930 and 1935, which seem to me to give inadequate support for the textual statements derived from them. Nor does he pay attention to the macro-economic multiplier effects of the sharp reduction in the marginal propensity to import manufactured goods, as is shown by Maizels' estimates. A proper evaluation of the role of the 1932 tariff (as distinct from that of the devaluation of sterling after September 1931) on the rapid economic growth in subsequent years calls for a more thorough investigation than it has hitherto received, particularly in the light of current controversies concerning the likely effect of import controls. See H. W. Richardson, 'The Tariff and Recovery', in *Economic Recovery in Britain, 1932–39* (London: Weidenfeld and Nicolson, 1967), and A. Maizels, *Growth and Trade* (Cambridge: Cambridge University Press, 1970) p. 136.

23. Originally published in four articles in *The Times* and in an expanded form as a pamphlet (now reprinted in *Collected Writings*, vol. IX, pp. 335–66).
24. Subject to a maximum quota of $450 million.
25. Italics not in original.
26. *The Autobiography of Bertrand Russell* (London: George Allen & Unwin, 1967) vol. I, pp. 71–2.

DISCUSSION

Official Discussant

Professor Donald Moggridge: I should like to thank Lord Kaldor for his interesting paper.

In his discussion, Lord Kaldor told us quite a bit about the sort of policy advice Keynes gave in the late 1920s and early 1930s. In what follows, I should like to do two things: first, to look a bit more closely at a subject really not touched on by Lord Kaldor—Keynes's success or lack thereof as a policy adviser during this period, and secondly to make a few comments on points in the paper where I think Lord Kaldor goes too far or is misleading.

In looking at this period, I think we must remember that Keynes was not, as he had been while at the Treasury between 1915 and 1919, an integral part of the Whitehall machine. He was rather, in varying degrees, an outsider who was trying to get his ideas into the policy-making machinery and was very often—in fact normally—unable to see whether his advice had any effect save in overt official policy measures. Also, it was not the case, as after 1939, that his strategic, if irregular, position within the machine was strengthened by the presence of disciples at various other key points in the system.

As a result, I think it would be fair to say that he was relatively unsuccessful in getting his advice adopted in the short term, unless his efforts at persuasion coincided to a considerable degree with the emergence of similar views at some strategic point within the machine. Good examples of such short-term successes include his recommendations for the management of sterling in 'Notes on the Currency Question' (November 1931), and the relative success of the Keynes–Henderson plan for international monetary reform.[1] Of course, he could also be successful over the longer term, as in the instances of his persuasion of the Treasury, largely through Sir Frederick Phillips, of the desirability of a counter-cyclical fiscal policy in 1937–8[2] and the creation of the climate of opinion in official circles that made cheap money compatible with war finance—i.e. the principle of the three per cent war.[3]

In fact, I think that one could convincingly argue that most of Keynes's inter-war successes in influencing the course of policy were results of longer-term persuasion—e.g. the peace treaties, the gold standard, monetary management etc.

Now why was he not more successful in the short term, always remembering that even during the year 1945, his influence, according to Professor Sayers,[4] 'never matched his brilliance on paper'? Here I think one can point to several causes.

The first was well brought out in a perceptive review of Keynes's *Essays in Persuasion*. There Leonard Woolf[5] suggested that one of the reasons for Keynes's failure lay in the 'ratio of his own cleverness to the average stupidity of distinguished persons who reach the top of the tree in practical affairs'. As he went on, 'There is a certain degree of stupidity which will no more mix with a certain degree of cleverness than oil with water. Stupid people are always suspicious of cleverness, but Mr. Keynes's kind of cleverness they regard as definitely indecent and immoral.' With Keynes this suspicion was heightened by his flexibility of mind which certainly created confusion over his views surrounding the return to gold in 1925;[6] saw him switch from supporting free trade to protection in 1929–31 and then away from protection after sterling left gold; saw him support public works between 1928 and 21 September 1931 and then drop the matter for the better part of a year. Nor was it diminished by his tendency to overstate his case, be it over the theoretical soundness of his *Treatise on Money*, or his claims for the power of scientific economic analysis in his case for setting up the Committee of Economists. Moreover, these characteristics tended to create real barriers against himself and his ideas, even when as during the Second World War informal contacts within the Whitehall machine might have eased matters, especially when Keynes entered a field in which the career experts were strangers to his ways.[7]

The second factor, which I have mentioned in passing, was also characteristic of Keynes as an investor. He was probably more successful, and more convincing, at long-term than short-term prophecies. But, as Leonard Woolf pointed out in the review I have mentioned, 'The politician ... is always thinking of what is going to happen next summer or winter [he could have said next week or next month], not of what is going to happen in three years time. To satisfy the politician you have to be a short-term prophet and to show that curious quality, political judgement, of which there is not much evidence in Mr Keynes's book.' Perhaps only in the Second World War could Keynes really reach towards his full potential as an adviser, for there, a mellower, more mature Keynes, could worry about short-term problems in a context where the longer-term post-war consequences of alternative solutions were important. Then also, in a world where the cry 'back to the good old pre-war days' carried little weight, he could also help to shape the post-war world.

But these are matters for more general discussion: they relate to this paper as well as the others this afternoon. In connection with Lord Kaldor's paper, I think there are two matters where the emphasis is slightly wrong.

First, in discussing the *Treatise* and Keynes's 'private evidence' to the Macmillan Committee, I think he has seriously underplayed an important link between the two which makes certain changes in Keynes's views more understandable. I am speaking of a distinction I have found useful in the past—that between the 'general case' and the 'special case' of the *Treatise.* In the 'general case', except in instances of income inflation where the monetary mechanism was 'singularly ill-adapted',[8] appropriate changes in the rate of interest could achieve price stability and full employment. However, in a world of fixed exchange rates—the regime which Keynes after extensive discussion of the pros and cons argued was most desirable[9]—an individual country, such as Britain, could face a dilemma. For in an international fixed exchange rate system with mobile international capital, a country might find itself in a position where its level of unit wage costs—Keynes called them efficiency wages—proved too high to allow it to achieve full employment at the existing level of international interest rates. In such a country, the monetary authorities could not use monetary policy to attain full employment because lower domestic interest rates would result in capital outflows and hence force the authorities either to reverse the policy or to abandon the exchange rate—which *in the circumstances of the time* meant abandoning the international standard. Therefore, what was needed were policy instruments that would raise investment at the existing rate of interest—e.g. public works—or insulate the domestic capital market from the international market—e.g. various restrictions on foreign lending—or make the domestic level of efficiency wages more compatible with those abroad—e.g. his tariff-subsidy proposal. Here was the justification for Keynes's whole programme for the Macmillan Committee and the Committee of Economists.[10]

Second, in discussing Keynes and protection and in ignoring this 'special case' of the *Treatise*, Lord Kaldor misses Keynes's intellectual consistency in abandoning both his public works and revenue tariff proposals after Britain left gold on 21 September 1931. For, in Keynes's view, with the exchange rate free to move they were unnecessary in the general framework of the *Treatise*. Of course, Keynes might *later* return to 'protectionism' as a means of gaining a certain freedom to experiment in methods of economic management, but this *later* view coincided with his abandonment of his *Treatise* on the way to the *General Theory*. However—and this seems to me to be the point of *The Means to Prosperity* (which was contemporaneous with 'National Self-Sufficiency') and Keynes's post-war 'package'—if the international community agreed to organise itself to encourage such experiments, even such protection *might* again prove unnecessary.

On a final point, I think Lord Kaldor's equation of protection and Britain's rapid recovery in 1930 is overdrawn on the basis of the *available* evidence. First of all, it ignores the effective depreciation of sterling, which was large until 1933 and remained significant until 1936.[11] Second, it ignores the fact that it seems almost impossible to relate inter-industry differences in performance during the years after 1931 to the widening net of British tariffs of 1931–2.[12] Perhaps the bases of Britain's recovery after 1932 and its continuance lay elsewhere.

NOTES

1. On the former, see Susan Howson, *Domestic Money Management in Britain, 1919–38* (Cambridge: Cambridge University Press, 1975) pp. 82–6 and appendix 4; and Susan Howson and Donald Winch, *The Economic Advisory Council, 1930–1939: A Study of Economic Advice during Depression and Recovery* (Cambridge: Cambridge University Press, 1977) pp. 100–4. On the latter, see ibid., pp. 115–21.
2. Ibid., pp. 128–32, 134–48.
3. Ibid., pp. 150–1; R. S. Sayers, *Financial Policy, 1939–1945* (London: HMSO, 1956) ch. V (iii).
4. Ibid., p. xiii.
5. L. Woolf, 'Keynessandra', *The New Statesman and Nation*, 19 December 1931.
6. See D. E. Moggridge, *British Monetary Policy, 1924–1931: The Norman Conquest of $4.86* (Cambridge: Cambridge University Press, 1972), especially ch. 3.
7. Mind you, even those used to him were sometimes ruffled. See, for example, the reaction of Sir Richard Hopkins to one war-time Keynes Treasury minute in *The Collected Writings of John Maynard Keynes*, vol. XXVII, p. 228.
8. *Collected Writings*, vol. V, pp. 243–7.
9. *Collected Writings*, vol. VI, pp. 348–64.
10. For a full elaboration of this view, see Howson and Winch, *Economic Advisory Council*, pp. 51ff.
11. J. Redmond, 'An Indicator of the Effective Exchange Rate for the Pound in the Nineteen Thirties', *Economic History Review*, 2nd series, XXXIII (I), February 1980.
12. The most extensive discussion of this issue is in H. W. Richardson, *Economic Recovery in Britain, 1932–39* (London: Weidenfeld & Nicolson, 1967) especially ch. 10 (II). In fact, Richardson goes on to argue the almost opposite case to Lord Kaldor's and to suggest (p. 255) that if iron and steel had not been protected 'productivity would have risen more'.

General Discussion

Professor Kaldor: I would like to make one point. I feel there was almost a conspiracy of silence about the effects of import duties introduced by Chamberlain and the Tory Government. All the intellectuals who have been interested to explore their effects have been thoroughly against and hostile to them. The only way they could satisfy themselves would be to show that protection was a complete failure and created a maldistribution of resources away from the law of comparative cost. They obviously couldn't do that because unemployment was falling and employment was rising. Manufacturing employment went up by 2 million, and total registered unemployment fell by 1.5 million from 3 million to 1.5 million. Therefore I feel I must take all the proofs to show that protection didn't do the trick with a pinch of salt. Also I do think, subject to correction, that Don Moggridge very much exaggerates the effects of going off the gold standard as a means of putting Britain in a very much better position with regard to imports and exports. After all, Roosevelt devalued with us to the same extent. He established a $4.86 rate by 1933, and many countries, before they formally abandoned the gold standard, gave such generous export subsidies and import duties to special accounts through the use of exchange control, that by 1935 very little remained to our competitive advantage. Now if you look at the industrial situation, recovery didn't really start until 1934. The best years were from 1935 up to September 1937 when there was a sudden cyclical setback. Take the steel industry. After the first war, the peak output of steel was 9 million, which fell to 5 million in 1932, and then in five years production increased to 13 million, an unprecedented rise in such a short space of time. I invite economic historians to re-examine this whole period if they can with less of the intellectual prejudices of nineteenth-century English liberalism.

Dr George Peden: May I, as an economic historian, respond to Professor Kaldor. First, I was surprised to hear Neville Chamberlain, who was Chancellor of the

Exchequer from the end of 1931 until 1937, being described by Professor Kaldor as perhaps the most successful Chancellor, or the most successful guide of Britain's economic fortunes, of the twentieth century. That is not a role Chamberlain is normally put into nowadays. Secondly, could I ask Lord Kaldor whether one can learn any lessons, as an economist, from a particular period in the past? There are two points here. Would other countries allow us to benefit today from protection and currency depreciation, as we benefited for a very short time in the early 1930s? Other countries ceased to allow us to benefit from such measures by the end of the 1930s, by which time we were negotiating mutual tariff reductions with the United States, and by which time the effective exchange rate of sterling, as measured against a 'basket' of leading currencies, was as high as it had been under the gold standard. That is one point. The other point is—can one draw analogies from a period when technology was somewhat different from today? Surely economies of scale in manufacturing are constantly increasing, and while the United Kingdom and the British Empire might have provided a sufficiently large market for individual industries in the 1930s, would the United Kingdom alone provide a sufficiently large market for the new forms of production in the 1980s?

Professor Kaldor: I am afraid it is not possible here to go into the pros and cons of import controls in the 1980s.

Sir Austin Robinson: I wonder whether I might add a few words to what both Professor Kaldor and Don Moggridge have said. I have never thought of Keynes in terms of being a short-term adviser or a long-term adviser. I think the remarkable thing about him is that he is still a relevant adviser fifty years later. I'm in the lucky position that Don Moggridge and Nicky Kaldor are also in of being in the middle of reading the proofs of the private evidence to the Macmillan Committee, and this is absolutely fascinating and will, I think, be completely necessary reading to anyone who is going to be teaching monetary theory in future. It is just as relevant today as it was then. But what I find particularly interesting here is that Keynes is looking at the institutions and trying to get clear as to how the institutions work. He is very dissatisfied with the fact that the same weapons are being used both to deal with the foreign balance and with the internal balance, and the conflicts between the two, and with the big problem of how you can find separate instruments that will work in the two separate fields without getting a conflict between the policies that you would want to adopt in the external field and those you would want to adopt in the internal field. This seems to me the very big contribution that he was making all through this time, and I think you can find plenty of other examples where Keynes's contribution (for example, at Bretton Woods and elsewhere) was in bringing to the surface the way that instruments were working and where they were working satisfactorily and where they were working very badly indeed and needed to be improved. I think that is Keynes's great contribution, and I regard that as much more important than whether he was exactly right about what ought to be happening within the next six months.

Dr Adrian Smith: In seeking to explain the reluctance of Labour's second administration to act upon Keynes's advice, it should perhaps be noted that several ministers remained suspicious of one so closely associated with Lloyd George's vociferous unemployment campaign of 1928–9. A single example may highlight a certain political naivety. Snowden's ill-health meant that he would be absent from the much-postponed discussion of the Economic Advisory Council's protectionist proposals planned for 12 March 1931. Keynes therefore sought to outflank the Treasury by forwarding MacDonald a proof copy of his forthcoming *New Statesman and Nation* paper on revenue tariffs; the Prime Minister could hardly have been amused to learn that a further copy had already been sent to the leader of the Liberal Party.

Dr Susan Howson: I feel I should take issue with Professor Kaldor, not about his views on Keynes as an economic adviser—there I can hardly disagree with him because a lot of what he had to say can be found in a book that I wrote with Donald Winch some years ago—but I do feel I have to say something about his views on the role of depreciation and monetary policy in the early 1930s. While I would agree with him that, if you want to look at the 1930s as a whole, the tariff probably was quite important in keeping recovery going, there is the point that the recovery began in the form of a housing boom in 1932 and this can be directly traced back to the cheap money policy for which depreciation, or at least the abandonment of the gold standard, was the necessary pre-condition. I think if one is looking at economic performance in the 1930s, this is something that has to be taken into account.

INTRODUCTION

Professor W. Hagenbuch (Chairman)

We now move on to the last period of Keynes's life as a policy adviser, the period of the Second World War. We are fortunate in having to address us on this topic Professor Thomas Wilson, Adam Smith Professor of Political Economy at the University of Glasgow since 1958. Not only is he the author of several works on planning, inflation, employment, growth and social policy but, more important for us today, he was in Whitehall during the war. Together with other economists, some of whom are here today, he was engaged in the business of economic planning for the war and for the peace. These economists were in various departments, but as one of them puts it 'brooding over the whole enterprise was the great Maynard Keynes himself at the Treasury'. Professor Wilson would, I believe, prefer not to be called a planner, but he has produced a good many plans in his time, and he has been economic consultant to both the government of Northern Ireland and the Secretary of State for Scotland. He is certainly an authority on planning, which means for him, as it did for Keynes, the regulation of the economy in order to maintain first and foremost stable prices and a high level of employment. The theme of Professor Wilson's address is planning for war and for the peace.

POLICY IN WAR AND PEACE: THE RECOMMENDATIONS OF J. M. KEYNES

Professor Tom Wilson

I Introduction

Over the past decade, Keynesian policies have been subjected to severe attack and there can be no doubt that Keynesianism has lost much ground—if ground can be measured by political and academic support. Today, when Keynesians are thus fighting a defensive action, it must be hard for members of a younger generation to appreciate the immense excitement that followed the publication of *The General Theory of Employment, Interest and Money* in 1936. It was a time of hope—hope that was to pervade the war-time discussion of post-war policies and was to remain strong for many years thereafter. It is true that, by 1936, a recovery from the worst depths of the Depression had taken place and this recovery owed little to expansionary fiscal policies of a Keynesian type; but it was also an incomplete recovery. Unemployment was still high and, even in 1937, the United States had barely regained its 1929 level of GNP when another downturn took place.

A different approach to policy seemed to be required. Admittedly, the measures recommended by Keynes were not altogether new in the sense of never having been propounded before. But the *General Theory* gave, or was believed to give, what had hitherto been lacking:

that is to say a firm and incontestable foundation for proposals that had previously been dismissed as heretical, eccentric and irresponsible. It was with these basic ideas that the *General Theory* was primarily concerned but the policy recommendations that seemed to follow were not presented in any detail in that work. Subsequently Keynes expounded his views in three articles in *The Times* for 12, 13 and 14 January 1937.[1]

War came before he had been able to do much more than this. As was to be expected, Keynes then responded quickly to the new situation and was soon applying his analytical mind to the problems of inflation, first as an academic economist and then as a government adviser. But the problems of peace were not neglected even in war-time and, within Whitehall, discussion of employment policy had already begun in 1941. Keynes, of course, played a leading part. Thus, when we turn our attention to Keynes's activities, we find him actively engaged in devising measures to deal both with the current war-time problems of inflation and scarcity on the one hand, and with the possible recurrence after the war of the deflationary pressures that were so much in his mind when he was writing the *General Theory*.

II War-time Inflation

It need scarcely be said that inflation was far from being a new topic for economists. Indeed it has been one of Keynes's complaints that economists had devoted too much attention to periods of rising prices and had tended to neglect unemployment, sometimes on the dubious ground that if booms could be prevented slumps would also be avoided. What was new about Keynes's approach was his use of national income accounts to analyse the prospective inflationary gap, and not only to analyse it but to estimate its probable magnitude. In doing so he was applying the theoretical approach of the *General Theory* with appropriate modifications, and was drawing upon the pioneering statistical work of Colin Clark and, later, of Richard Stone.

In two articles in *The Times* (14 and 15 November 1939) and in his pamphlet *How to Pay for the War* (1940) Keynes presented his estimates of potential output and of the probable claims upon it. An inflationary gap was to be anticipated. How best could it be dealt with?

The problem would be eased and the size of gap lessened by a rise in voluntary saving. But 'saving' is a tricky concept. If more money was created and more was spent than the flow of goods available at constant prices, then prices would rise if allowed to do so and the bulk of the population would be forced to consume less in real terms. Profits would be swollen but the few who received these inflated profits would have a high propensity to save and, in war-time conditions, would also have small inclination to spend on capital goods. Thus the shift in the distribution of income would bring about an initial voluntary reduction in private expenditure, but this would not be a stable position. For, after a lag, wages would be forced upwards and a foolish inflationary spiral would then ensue.[2]

The more voluntary saving that could be encouraged the better, without relying on this distributional twist, but it was not to be expected that the emergence of a serious inflationary gap could be prevented. Demand might then be held back by rationing, but rationing could not be comprehensive and demand would thus be diverted to what was not rationed. There should, indeed, be an iron ration of essentials combined with price controls. This was crucially important but would not, by itself, suffice.

'The general character of our solution', he wrote '... must be, therefore, that it withdraws from expenditure a proportion of the increased earnings' (that would be engendered in the war-time economy). This must be done by taxation and there was no escape from the fact that additional taxation would fall on the population as a whole; it was statistically impossible to make the rich alone pay for the war. Taxation was required but there should be a new element in the tax structure: deferred tax credits. Part of the additional tax contribution should, in effect, take the form of a compulsory loan which would be repaid at an appropriate stage after the war when this repayment would help to prevent the slump that was then to be anticipated.[3]

In crude summary this was the essence of Keynes's proposal. He held that, in this way, the war-time burden would do less harm by reducing incentives and weakening morale. There should, he claimed, be no permanent reduction in the standard of living of the working class—a bold claim that depended upon the way in which the post-war repayments would be financed.[4] What *is* true is that the workers would be better off that way than with uncontrolled inflation leading to profiteering. Whether their position would be significantly better than without tax credits is not obvious.

Did this scheme really have a significant effect on the war economy? The answer must surely be in the negative. In part this was because the scheme as adopted by Kingsley Wood in the 1941 Budget was on only about a quarter of the scale Keynes had recommended. If it had been more fully adopted, would it have been possible to raise total taxation, including that backed by post-war credits, to a still higher level? If so there would have been less market pressure on the controls. It is not clear, however, that deferred tax credits, even on a larger scale, would have had as big an effect on morale as Keynes, for his part, anticipated. It may be the case that, apart from a few intellectuals and a few economists, not many people were inclined to put so much trust in Treasury promises of post-war repayment as to be influenced in their war-time conduct thereby! Such scepticism certainly proved to be justified in the event, for the credits were not repaid for a long time after the war and then only in heavily depreciated currency. Whether the device was worth using once may be debated; it would certainly be difficult to use it again.

The pamphlet, *How to Pay for the War*, greatly interested economists at the time and there may still be an inclination to suppose that the scheme there propounded constituted Keynes's main contribution to the effective running of the war economy. That, of course, would not be so. On the international side he took a leading part in the Lend–Lease negotiations on which so much depended and, more generally, was actively concerned with external financial matters throughout the war. On the domestic side, there was no other 'Keynes Plan', in addition to the post-war credit plan; but his influence was not restricted to his devising of such labelled schemes. The war was run with a much greater regard for fairness than had been the case in the First World War. The iron ration of basic foodstuffs, the more flexible points system for other foods and the system of clothes rationing with lines of partially-standardised production—all these measures went a long way to ensure fair shares. Price control and subsidies held down the cost-of-living. Of course there were black markets, but these were less important than would have been the case if fiscal policy had been slacker. It would be wrong, admittedly, to leave the impression that planning was based essentially on estimates of national output and the claims upon it. That was not so. The war effort was organised largely by means of quantitative plans for production with estimates—sometimes rather rough estimates—of the requirements for manpower, shipping, raw materials and so on. These plans were enforced substantially by means of direct controls. Keynes, for his part, took no direct part in this kind of physical planning. Indeed, he was not a member of either of the two crucially important committees, the Manpower Committee and the Shipping Committee. But it is also necessary to make the point that if inflationary pressure had been stronger, it could have weakened the effectiveness of this kind of planning in physical terms if financial policy had been more lax. Although finance seemed to play a very subsidiary role, the physical and the financial aspects were in fact interlocked in a whole variety of ways.[5] It is hard to assess the extent to which Keynes was involved in all this, even with the *Collected Writings* at hand. It may be a reasonable inference that those contributions by Keynes which did not bear a visible Keynes 'trade mark' were at least as substantial as those that did.

I have made no mention so far of an important aspect of war finance for which we do know that Keynes was partly responsible. This was a cheap-money war. Keynes was quite insistent that it should be so. As early as 28 September 1939, he had maintained in a letter to *The Times* that the Treasury should not borrow at more than 2½ per cent and he continued to advise along these lines. There was not, I think, much opposition to a cheap-money war, but Hicks rightly gave a warning in a letter to Keynes of 4 October 1939: 'Although I am quite in agreement with you about the *pros* of keeping interest rates down during the war, I cannot help feeling that that policy has the considerable disadvantage of piling up liquid funds in the hands of the public, which is likely to make the problem of controlling the post-war boom even more intractable.' Keynes did not agree. He did not think effective demand after the war would be much affected by the terms on which it was borrowed during the war—thus missing Hicks's point that with very low war-time interest rates more capital would be held in short-term liquid assets and in cash. In the event, the suppressed inflation of war-time left for post-war a problem of pent-up demand backed by accumulated purchasing power, as Hicks had anticipated. Keynes was inclined to underestimate this danger for another reason. At that stage he was anticipating only a short war[6] to be followed by a short boom which might 'only be an event of a few months'.[7] He was later to modify his views about the probable length of the boom, as we shall see when we turn to his work on post-war policies; but he remained a cheap-money man to the end.

III Post-war Policies: Social Security

Even in the early days of the war, Keynes was already directing some attention to the probable requirements of the post-war period. What now seems a rather odd example is to be found in the first section of volume XXVII of the *Collected Writings* which deals with the anticipated accumulation of stocks of primary products in some of the main producing countries and the possible use of these surpluses for post-war relief. A special section of the Ministry of Economic Warfare was charged with exploring the possibilities, and Keynes took part in the interdepartmental discussions which, of course, involved the Treasury. It has to be borne in mind that many people, including Keynes, had initially anticipated a short war. Its prolongation and the various changes in the areas affected were soon to strip these investigations of whatever interest they may have had. Work on the more general problems of commodity markets was to continue, however, and to be reflected in the discussion of post-war policies, in so far as this related to buffer-stock and commodity-stabilisation schemes. Keynes's interest was therefore sustained and his flow of comments and suggestions continued. These matters cannot, however, be further explored in the present paper. Let us turn, then, to domestic policy.

In June 1941, Beveridge was invited to review the existing arrangements for social security and to suggest amendments where these seemed appropriate. As his work progressed, however, he began to formulate a new scheme for comprehensive social security and this was to become a topic of lively debate in Whitehall. Some difference of opinion was to be expected about the proper form and scope of a social security scheme but the central issue of debate was the extent to which government should commit itself. Most of its members were preoccupied with the task of fighting the war. Look, if you will, at the minutes published as appendices to Churchill's memoirs and consider the extraordinary range of decisions relating to the war with which he had to deal. It is amazing that he had *any* time and energy to devote to post-war problems. In such circumstances it would not have been unreasonable to hold that, although the formulation of post-war policies might continue, financial commitments should not be accepted. The case for caution was strengthened at this time by the sharp difference of opinion between two of the leading economic advisers: H. D. Henderson, on the one hand, who was deeply pessimistic about post-war prospects, and Keynes, on the other, who took a more sanguine view. Once again the national income accounts were put to what was, in those days, a comparatively novel use, for estimates were projected forward on various assumptions to a hypothetical post-war year, and this procedure allowed the differences between the contestants to be presented in quantitative form. In the event, Keynes was, on balance, the winner, for the Cabinet was persuaded to accept the greater part of what Beveridge had recommended.[8]

Of the many issues raised in the course of this debate, two are of particular interest because of the relationship they bear to Keynes's views on post-war macro-economic policy. The first was his emphasis on the importance of making it clear that 'it is not intended in future to put the benefits and the contributions on a cost of living sliding scale, but only to make adjustments when there have been major disturbances, as, for example, between pre-war values and probable post-war values.[9] This was also Beveridge's own view.[10] Neither Beveridge nor Keynes had a remotely adequate anticipation of the inflationary pressures that have persisted for many years since the war, but both believed that indexation would weaken the resistance to inflation.[11]

The second point to be noted here is that Keynes believed strongly, as Beveridge did, in financing social security by hypothecated contributions. He conceded that the proposed social insurance fund is 'admittedly, to some extent, a fiction. Certainly it is not a fund in any actuarial sense.'[12] As the former chairman of an insurance company he could scarcely say otherwise! There were, however, two reasons why he believed in earmarked contributions. First, this method of finance would make clear to people what they were paying for—a point that had been much stressed by Beveridge.

Secondly, it was not desirable that current payments and current contributions should always balance, but the surpluses and deficits that would thus appear would not be allowed to disturb the balance of the Chancellor's ordinary budget. He held, therefore, that: 'The social security budget should be one section of a capital or long-term budget.... For the ordinary budget should be balanced at all times.'[13] Thus he was fitting the social security proposals into what he regarded as the appropriate framework for post-war stabilisation policy.

IV Post-war Policies: Maintaining Employment

Within Whitehall, work on *employment policy* began at an early stage. In February 1941, James Meade had prepared a memorandum on the subject and this was the start of prolonged discussions between the Economic Section, under Lionel Robbins, to which Meade belonged, the Treasury with Keynes and Henderson again at odds, the Ministry of Reconstruction under Greenwood and the Prime Minister's Statistical Branch under Cherwell.

The outcome was the White Paper on Employment Policy (Cmd. 6520) which appeared on the very eve of the Second Front in May 1944. It was an exceedingly important state paper for, in it, a British Government accepted for the first time the obligation to try to maintain 'a high and stable level of employment'. The means proposed for the attainment of this objective were set out and were soon attacked as being too cautious. The proposals did not go far enough to satisfy the critics and it was rumoured that Keynes had been only partly successful in getting his recommendations accepted. It is a belief that has persisted. Thus, in 1969,

Donald Winch could say that 'the chief weakness of the White Paper lay in its treatment of the budget as a means of controlling the level of employment. The paragraphs dealing with this subject are highly confused. The main remedies proposed, contra-cyclical public investment programmes and variations in national insurance contributions, were both outside the framework of normal budgeting.'[14] With the official papers not then available Winch could not have been aware that these very aspects of the White Paper reflected Keynes's own views! Therefore, on the basis of the evidence then available to Winch, it was reasonable to infer that '...if Keynes's views had prevailed the document would have been much better'.[15] As we shall see, the evidence now available leads to a somewhat different verdict.

Keynes had given broad indications of his position in *The General Theory of Employment, Interest and Money*, and had been more explicit in articles contributed to *The Times* in 1937, mentioned above. Then in 1942 he explained his general position in a broadcast: 'Here is a real problem, fundamental yet essentially simple, which it is important for all of us to try to understand. The first task is to make sure that there is enough demand to provide employment for everyone. The second task is to prevent a demand in excess of the physical possibilities of supply, which is the proper meaning of inflation.'[16] Simple indeed—over-simple in the light of experience, for there is no hint here of the problems of stagflation. Let us, however, leave that formidable complication aside for the moment and direct our attention to the ways in which Keynes believed these basic objectives could be achieved.

The first point to observe is his discarding in the *General Theory* of a technique of stabilisation on which he had laid great stress five years earlier in *A Treatise on*

Money (1931). This was the manipulation of long-term interest rates in order to offset fluctuations in the expected return on investment. His abandonment of this recommendation followed from his liquidity preference theory which can be detected in the *Treatise on Money* but became a central feature of his analysis in the *General Theory*. If the complex of bond yields depends upon liquidity preference, given the amount of money, and if liquidity preference is based on past experience, then it may be hard to get bond yields down sufficiently to check a recession if previously raised to halt a boom. In his *Times* articles of 1937, Keynes held that dear money must be avoided 'as we would hell-fire'. It was true that some investment should be held back during a recovery to prevent excess demand. 'But we must find other means of achieving this than a higher rate of interest. For if we allow the rate of interest to be affected, *we cannot easily reverse the trend*' [italics added].

What he was postulating was, in effect, a bond-yield ratchet, in addition to the money-wage ratchet. Why a ratchet? If past experience of high yields makes it hard to lower yields, would past experience of low yields not make it hard to raise them? The apparent asymmetry could be explained in Keynesian terms by saying that to keep bond prices up in face of official sales, people would have to run down their liquid balances (M_2) which are limited;[17] in the opposite circumstances, however, they would allow these balances to grow indefinitely. We may note in passing that Keynes was here conceding nothing to the 'Pigou effect,' although he himself had suggested an effect of this kind to Denis Robertson in the mid-1920s.[18]

For Keynes, the crucial point was to be in a position to keep rates down, for the long-run prospect was a saturation of investment opportunities with the return on investment falling to a very low figure.[19] It is true that even an indefinitely sustained cheap-money policy could not ensure that there would be no liquidity trap; but the trap would be located on a lower contour of bond rates if bond prices were not allowed to fall even in order to restrain a boom. This was so because spells of dear money would inflate the generally held idea of what could be regarded as the 'safe' bond yield below which increased liquidity would be prudent.

So far I have referred deliberately to the stabilisation of bond yields without claiming that Keynes wanted to provide a fully elastic supply of money. In fact there are some passages which suggest that he did not. Thus: 'Changes in the complex of interest rates, with a view to controlling the trade cycle and to offset inflationary or deflationary trends, should not be precluded but should affect the shorter-term rather than the longer-term issues, and should, as a rule, be regarded as secondary to the technique of rationing the volume, rather than altering the terms of credit.'[20] That is to say, increases in short-term rates would sometimes be appropriate but higher long-term rates never. How the two markets, the short and the long, were to be so segregated is not made clear and his proposal for their separation is all the more odd because in the *Treatise* he had confidently maintained that important changes in the former would be quickly transmitted to the latter. Thus there is a puzzle here and perhaps a contradiction. But it cannot be doubted that interest-rate policy was accorded at most a minor role by Keynes when the *Treatise* had been left behind. He did not hold, however, as some neo-Keynesians are wont to do, that the supply of money should completely accommodate changes in demand; short-rates would sometimes rise and, in particular, the other conditions on which funds were provided should be tightened up—that is to say direct control rather than control by interest rates.

The White Paper on employment policy accords some role to monetary policy but makes the familiar point that changes in interest rates may be more effective in checking a boom than in curing a slump (paras 59 and 60). The need for fiscal measures was therefore held to be established. It did not necessarily follow from this reasoning that dear money should be avoided in a boom when monetary policy could be effected. The theory of liquidity preference was needed to bring the smell of hell-fire that so troubled Keynes.

It is true that Keynes was not as much concerned with controlling booms as with preventing depressions, but he did not challenge the general assumption that the war would be followed by a potentially inflationary boom. Early in the war, he had expected this phase to be short, but by May 1943 he was suggesting five years.[21] Meade thought Keynes's estimate too long.[22] How should this prospective inflation be contained? Not in Keynes's view by higher interest rates. A cheap-money war was to be followed by a cheap-money peace. Continuity would be preserved right through the post-war inflation with, for example, 10-year bonds issued at 3 per cent (not quite Dalton's policy but a long way towards it). Excess private demand would be held back essentially as in war-time by taxation and by direct controls over private expenditure; public investment would be carefully phased. It must be admitted, however, that his account of the measures he favoured was brief and sadly inadequate. There appears to be little perception, in his comments, of the difficulty of maintaining direct controls in peace-time—difficulties which reflect both the increasing diversity of the output demanded and the increasing reluctance of the public to submit to controls. In particular the manpower budget, which had been of central importance in war-time, could not be expected to operate in the same way in peace-time. There is no evidence that Keynes devoted much attention to such considerations and this was unfortunate for, had he done so, he might have appreciated more fully the dangers of the high liquidity likely to accompany cheap money, and therefore the case for a financial policy that could be used in tandem with the remaining but increasingly less effective direct controls.

The truth is that Keynes's real interest lay not in the post-war inflationary period but, (a) in a period of normal potential instability which he expected to follow, and (b) in another period—perhaps ten to twenty years ahead—when a secular insufficiency of expenditure would manifest itself unless prevented by appropriate policy.[23] Let us now direct attention to period (a), a period of potential cyclical instability with no marked trend as yet towards chronic deflation.

The method for preventing instability on which he laid most stress was the stabilisation of investment. It was true that a country might import its instability but 'the proportion of investment represented by the balance of trade, which is not easily brought under short-term control, may be smaller than before'.[24] He goes on: 'The main task should be to *prevent* large fluctuations by a stable long-term programme.' Changes in public investment, if appropriate in timing and amount, would offset variations in private investment. The traditional remedy of public works could thus be expanded and dignified as a policy for public investment. Secondly, means could be found of making industrial investment itself more stable. 'If two-thirds or three-quarters of total investment is carried out or can be influenced by public or semi-public bodies, a programme of a stable character should be capable of reducing the potential range of fluctuations to much narrower limits than formerly.' As we have observed, interest-rate policy was not to be used to this end and Keynes was not at all explicit about the way in which other techniques could be employed when controls had largely been removed with the ending of the post-war boom. Meade threw out some suggestions in a letter to Keynes, 3 June 1943, but he had already warned Keynes that, in the view of the Economic Section, control might not be easy.[25] In the White Paper, there is a hint of an arrangement by which firms might accumulate tax-credits in good years that could be used in bad years—a technique that was developed most fully in Sweden.

There is another and more basic criticism of Keynes's treatment of investment. Rather too often in his writings Keynes treated investment as though its primary function was to serve as a channel for the disbursement of purchasing power. Of course it would be absurd, quite absurd, to suggest that he overlooked the other functions of investment; but this particular one was so much in his thoughts that the others sometimes sank out of sight. There is, however, a warning in the White Paper (paras 61–2) that there are limits to the extent to which investment can be, or should be, controlled for the sake of stability. Post-war experience was to underline the fact that the loss in other respects cannot be lightly disregarded. Those responsible for investment in electricity supply, in public transport, in coal-mining and so on, are naturally resentful when their investment programmes are warped in order to serve macro-economic objectives. Even if their objections are over-ruled, there will be lags before significant changes can be made, as Christopher Dow was to demonstrate on the basis of early post-war experience.[26]

If we now turn to industrial investment we find that Keynes's treatment was much less adequate than might be expected in view of the weight he attached to it. Indeed, the treatment of investment in the *General Theory* has long been regarded as one of its weakest parts. What is particularly puzzling and regrettable is the fact that his views on investment did not reflect more adequately the work of his close colleague, D. H. Robertson. Robertson believed that industrial investment was bound to fluctuate because technical change came in spurts. Such innovational investment could not be stabilised without sacrificing growth, but secondary waves of rising or receding expenditure might be avoided by appropriate policies. Whether or not the whole of Robertson's theory is held to be applicable today, it is clear that he appreciated the possible tension between the different functions performed by investment expenditure.

There can be no serious doubt that, notwithstanding all the difficulties just mentioned, useful measures can be taken to reduce the instability of total investment. That this is the case seems clear enough when we reflect upon the folly of cutting public investment at a time when private investment was severely depressed—as in the early 1930s—and when there was no stagflation to complicate the situation. The question is whether such measures are likely to suffice. In particular, would the effectiveness of public action not be greatly fortified by anti-cyclical variations in the budget which might now be in deficit, now move into surplus?

As observed above, Keynes wanted to have two budgets, a current budget, and a capital budget, and '*the ordinary budget should be balanced at all times*'.[27] It has also been observed that the caution of the White Paper on employment policy has generally been regarded as evidence of a failure by Keynes to get his way in Whitehall. One of the sentences that seemed to justify this inference may be quoted here: 'None of the proposals contained in this Paper involves deliberate planning for a deficit in the National Budget in years of sub-normal trade activity' (para. 74). In reality this was Keynes's *own* view.

The 'ordinary' or 'national' budget would cover all current expenditure on goods and services and all transfers other than social security transfers which were to be included in the capital budget. Receipts would consist of the proceeds of all taxation other than social security contributions.

If taxes were lowered, it would be hard to raise them again. If deficits were proposed, the proposal would provoke opposition and perhaps weaken confidence—a possibility that was recognised in the *General Theory*. There was, however, another reason for Keynes's opposition which provokes quite basic questions about his theoretical position. This was his scepticism about the possibility of affecting consumers' expenditure in the short run.

Before dealing with this point we must first note an omission. The current budget could be put out of balance in either direction by changes in the consumption expenditure of the public authorities without corresponding changes in taxation. There is some guarded speculation about the possibility of such variations in the White Paper of 1944; but Keynes does not seem to have been much interested. It was on *private* consumption that he expressed his views so clearly—and the surprising fact is that he was highly sceptical about what could be done to alter such expenditure by changes in taxation. 'I doubt', he says 'if much is to be hoped from proposals to offset unforeseen short-period fluctuations in investment by stimulating short-period changes in consumption.' This view is not to be explained by saying that direct taxation, as he investigated in the 1940s, would be paid mainly by the rich whose propensity to save was low. For he referred also quite specifically to indirect taxes. He had other reasons for his scepticism.[28] The point he stressed was that consumption is likely to be unresponsive to changes in disposable income in the short run. In some sentences of the recently published papers, he is anticipating the theory of permanent income to be developed much later by Friedman. Thus: 'People have established standards of life. Nothing will upset them more than to be subject to pressure constantly to vary them up and down.'[29] It has long been recognised in the literature of the Keynesian school that the marginal propensity to consume may be lower in the short run than in the long run; but Keynes himself had carried the argument much further in these official papers by maintaining that the marginal propensity to consume is so low in the short period as to make counter-cyclical changes in personal taxation of little value. What then becomes of the theory of the multiplier which he continued to stress? Perhaps an attempt at reconciliation might be made by suggesting that consumers will respond more to a change in income obtained by getting employment than to a change brought about by lower taxation; for the former may be thought to be more lasting than the latter. Whether or not this is thought to be a convincing line, it is not the line Keynes took.

There is, however, another puzzle here. For, as we have seen, Keynes *did* come down strongly in support of counter-cyclical fluctuations in social security contributions. Even without such variations, the social security system is, of course, a built-in stabiliser (of expenditure). Meade's proposal to vary the contribution rates with variations in unemployment was designed to create a super built-in stabiliser. But the effect of changing the employee's contribution will come through only if income receivers adjust their consumption when disposable income changes. By endorsing Meade's proposal, Keynes accepted this implication,[30] but did not explain how it could be reconciled with his view, expressed in the rejecting of the case for cuts in other taxes, that the short-run marginal propensity to consume was very small. Why should people respond in this way only to changes in the social security contribution?

At this point it may be tempting to speculate that Keynes was placing his faith in variations in the *emloyer's* contribution rather than the *employee's*. For the employer's contribution not only reduces cash flow but is seen as a discriminatory tax on employment. In fact, however, Keynes attached little or no importance to changes in the employer's payroll tax and even tried to persuade Meade to confine his recommendation to the employee's contribution.

There is no escape from the conclusion that Keynes had got into a muddle over all this. Nor is there any escape from the conclusion that the limitations of the White Paper, so much stressed by its critics, are to be largely explained by the fact that Keynes's own views, far from having been over-ridden, had actually prevailed. It would perhaps be natural to suppose that the Economic Section, under Robbins, would be more cautious than Keynes. But the Economic Section's proposals, as presented by Meade, had been favourable to counter-cyclical changes in other taxes and dubious about the usefulness of having a current budget and a capital budget.[31] There was also support for a bolder tax policy from the Prime Minister's statistical branch. Of course there were other sceptics as well as Keynes; but the fact remains that the caution of the White Paper was not inconsistent with Keynes's own position.

Keynes was also cautious in his estimates of the

minimum level to which unemployment could be reduced.[32] Writing in *The Times* at the beginning of 1937 he had said: 'It is natural to interject that it is premature to abate our efforts to increase employment so long as the figures of unemployment remain so large. But I believe we are approaching, or have reached, the point where there is not much advantage in applying a further general stimulus at the centre.' At that time unemployment was about 10 per cent on a modern basis of reckoning—higher, therefore, than in 1980! It should not be inferred, of course, that Keynes was *satisfied* with unemployment at that level. For it could, he believed, be brought down by measures to deal with structural problems. Thus: 'We are more in need today of a rightly distributed demand than of a greater aggregate demand. But he went on to add that '*the Treasury would be entitled to economise elsewhere to compensate for the cost of special assistance to the distressed areas*' [italics added].

The war itself was to bring about large structural changes and Keynes strongly recommended that structural policies should be maintained after the war. In June 1943, he came down in favour of 5 per cent as the *average* figure to be aimed at. Presumably this would imply a lower figure in good years but he did not offer a guess about dispersion around the average.[33] He was, however, sceptical about Beveridge's 3 per cent, given in *Full Employment in a Free Society* (1944). Thus in a letter to Beveridge he said: 'No harm in aiming at 3 per cent unemployment, but I shall be surprised if we succeed.'[34] As things turned out, unemployment was to be well below even Beveridge's average for a quarter of a century after the war, and any suggestion that it was too low provoked an indignant reply. Thus when the Commission on Incomes and Prices suggested in 1962 that unemployment might be allowed to rise above its current figure, about 2 per cent, it was fiercely denounced by many who regarded themselves as Keynesians! The Commission may well have been right but it is also surely the case that Keynes's 5 per cent was too high for that period—and would have been considered so by some economists who did not claim to be fully committed Keynesians.

Keynes's high figure for unemployment has an indirect bearing on another issue, the difficulties of fine-tuning. Fine-tuning was not a problem of immediate concern in the early 1930s when there was a desperate need to raise expenditure and no immediate danger of overdoing it. In the 1940s, however, Keynes was stressing the desirability of devising policies that would prevent slumps, rather than simply cure them, and this required the *stabilising* of expenditure (more correctly it should be the rate of growth of expenditure relatively to the growth of potential output, but Keynes did not normally express his views in terms appropriate to a growing economy). Such stabilisation would seem to call for the fine-tuning that is so hard to achieve. Keynes, for his part, had little conception of these difficulties but is not open to serious criticism on that account. For the use of the national accounts in the formulation and execution of policy was still a new technique with both its potentialities and its limitations unknown. There is, however, a question as to how stable expenditure had to be to achieve the aim of 'stability'. *Some* dispersion was clearly contemplated by Keynes, by Meade and also by Beveridge—indeed a good deal more than was acceptable in the 1950s and 1960s. The fineness of the tuning that was attempted was very fine indeed—far more so than anything Keynes had in mind. It would be roughly true to say that we came to attach as much importance to a variation of 0.1 per cent in unemployment as Keynes attached to a variation of 1 per cent. It should be recalled that the scheme for varying social security contributions which Keynes strongly supported contemplated fluctuations in unemployment that would have been thought intolerable after the war. The variable contribution rates referred to brackets of 2 per cent in unemployment. The lowest range with the highest contribution was under 5 per cent; the highest over 11 per cent.

As we have recorded, Keynes expected a growing long-term deflationary pressure as investment opportunities became exhausted—phase (b) above. This forecast of secular stagnation had been made in the *General Theory* but did not really follow from the central core of the analysis. Additional highly speculative assumptions were needed to sustain it and these have proved so far to be singularly inappropriate. Keynes thought it would be necessary to stimulate consumption and discourage saving; the emphasis has rather been on the need to foster relatively more investment and therefore more saving. We need not go on to discuss the various aspects of this theory of stagnation, but it is important to record that Keynes's attachment to it may have served to distract his attention from the very different problems of avoiding or curing inflation.

In some notes written just before his death in April 1946, Keynes said: 'We have been using "inflation" to mean pressure of demand to raise prices above current cost of production, e.g. in Budget Speech. Quite a useful practice. But inflation of this sort is a temporary factor, I think, and one we have learned to keep under good control.'[35] Inflation had indeed been suppressed fairly effectively in war-time in the sense that the inflationary gap had been prevented by an elaborate system of rationing and controls from having the effect it would otherwise have had on the price level. It can fairly be said, however, that Keynes was over-optimistic about the ease with which inflation could be controlled in peace-time by fiscal methods, unsupported by such regulations or by restrictions on the rate of growth of the money supply.

Keynes was, it is true, somewhat apprehensive lest sustained full employment in peace-time led to wage-inflation. In the White Paper it was firmly laid down that: 'The level of prices must be kept reasonably stable' (para. 39). The 'joint efforts of the Government, employers and organized labour' should be directed to this end. There is, however, no recommendation in favour of an incomes policy, merely an exhortation that 'Workers must examine their trade practices and customs to ensure that they do not constitute a serious impediment to an expansionist economy and so defeat the object of a full employment policy' (para. 53). The employers, too, must seek in 'larger output rather than higher prices the reward of enterprise and good management'. The White Paper went on to recommend that government should take action against restrictive practices by employers but there is no suggestion of official action against the unions[36]—a marked asymmetry that was to characterise public policy for many years and does so today in the sense that action against the union monopolists is still very mild (1980).

It is a reasonable inference that Keynes broadly accepted what the White Paper had to say on these matters. It is true that in 1926 he had strongly denounced the trade unions: 'There are the *Trade-Unionists*, once the oppressed, now the tyrants, whose selfish and sectional pretensions need to be bravely opposed.'[37] There is, however, no similar statement to be found in his writings on policy for the period after the Second World War and we do not know how far he would have endorsed measures to prevent the abuse of power by the unions. Would he have favoured an incomes policy? We know that he disliked controls and it is hard to believe that he would have supported proposals for the detailed and permanent control of industry. But the term 'incomes policy' has many meanings. Perhaps he would have lent his support to one or another of the more liberal versions, but this can only be speculation. What can be said with confidence, however, is that wage inflation would have been much less if unemployment had been interpreted to mean an average of about 5 per cent.

I have concentrated attention in this paper on domestic policies, as required to do by my remit from the organisers of this conference. In doing so, I have also been reflecting the principal contents of volume XXVII of the *Collected Writings*. (The main exception is the earlier part of the volume on commodity policy.) A brief word must, however, be added about his views of international trade and finance. Much of the time and effort of his last years was devoted to the establishment of new international institutions and the devising of appropriate rules of behaviour for a liberal economic order. Although the Bretton Woods agreement did not give him as much as he had asked, he was optimistic. In particular, he was pleased by the scarce currency clause in the constitution of the IMF (article VII). These new international measures and the new measures for maintaining employment would complement and support each other. In these circumstances he abandoned his old protectionist attitude and was sharply critical of those who advocated protection by means of high tariffs, import controls and discrimination. The anti-liberal proposals which came both from right-wing Tories and left-wing Socialists must be rejected. Thus he wrote to Kalecki in December 1944 to express admiration of *The Economics of Full Employment* (Oxford: Blackwell, 1944)—a collection of papers sponsored by the Oxford Institute of Statistics. But he went on to say: 'The one exception I make to this, as perhaps you have guessed, is the section on International Aspects.... What is happening to Balogh? He has done some excellent stuff in the past, but much of what I have seen of his lately strikes me as extremely confused.'[38]

In June 1944, he wrote to Professor Hayek about the latter's *Road to Serfdom*: 'In my opinion a grand book ... you will not expect me to accept quite all the economic dicta in it. But morally and philosophically I find myself in agreement with virtually the whole of it.... One point which you might perhaps have pressed further is the tendency to disparage the profit motive while still depending on it and putting nothing in its place.' But he firmly repudiated the view that 'as soon as one moves in the planned direction you are necessarily launched on the slippery path which will lead you in due course over the precipice'. He differed radically from Hayek on this issue, just as he differed from the more doctrinaire Left. 'Reading the *New Statesman and Nation* one sometimes feels that those who write there, while they cannot safely oppose moderate planning, are really hoping in their hearts that it will not succeed; and so prejudice more violent action.' He himself had no doubt that 'Moderate planning will be safe if those carrying it out are rightly orientated in their own minds and hearts to the moral issue.'[39]

This was his own basic position throughout. A freer society must be preserved. He had no sympathy for communism which was, in his view, not only oppressive but inefficient. (Although I can find no reference to the most tragic example of such inefficiency, the terrible Russian famine of 1933, which coincided with the world slump, he can scarcely have been unaware of it.) The communist path was to be rejected. So was extreme *laissez-faire*, especially at a time of mass unemployment. In the *General Theory* he had written: 'It is certain that the world will not tolerate much longer the unemployment which, apart from brief intervals of excitement, is associated—and in my mind inevitably associated—with present day capitalistic individualism. But it may be possible by a right analysis of the problem to cure the disease whilst preserving efficiency and freedom' (p. 381). We had a very long period of 'excitement' after the war; but it is over now, and with its passing Keynes's message is once more directly relevant to the needs of our society.

NOTES

1. Reprinted in T. W. Hutchison, *Keynes v. the Keynesians?* (Institute of Economic Affairs, 1977).
2. See chapter 2 of *How to Pay for the War* (London: Macmillan, 1940). We may note in passing that his analysis at this point was very similar to earlier theories of forced savings, notably that developed by D. H. Robertson in 'Industrial Fluctuation and the Natural Rate of Interest', *Economic Journal* (1934), reprinted in *Essays in Monetary Theory* (London: P. S. King and Son, 1940); see also T. Wilson, 'Robertson, Money and Monetarism', *Journal of Economic Literature* (Dec. 1980). Keynes himself had subjected the theory of forced savings to exaggerated and undiscriminating condemnation in the *General Theory*.
3. It may be of interest to record an incident not mentioned in vol. xxvii of the *Collected Writings*. A proposal for post-war credits was also put forward by Professor H. O. Meredith of Queen's University, Belfast, who had been a Fellow of King's and a contemporary of Keynes. Meredith sent his article to Keynes as editor of the *Economic Journal* but Keynes returned it, a little curtly perhaps, on the grounds that he was about to publish an article of his own on this subject—an article which was to appear in the issue for 1939. Meredith's paper appeared in the *Political Quarterly* in 1940 and, I suspect, attracted no attention. It is true that Keynes had worked out a more elaborate scheme which made use of the national income statistics. One might perhaps have expected a reference by Keynes to Meredith's paper. Its omission was presumably a regrettable oversight, not an uncharacteristic lack of generosity on Keynes's part. The omission, was, however, the more surpris-

ing in view of their friendly correspondence just after the publication of the *General Theory* when Meredith sent Keynes some shrewd and perceptive comments (*Collected Writings*, vol. XXIX, pp. 211–13).

4. Keynes was not sufficiently explicit on this last point. Whenever repaid, expenditure by recipients of the credits would be a claim on current output in that period. If, as a result of repayment, output was larger because the deflationary pressures were offset in this way, and would not have been offset in any other way, then it would follow that, to this extent, neither the workers nor indeed the rest of society would have made a permanent sacrifice. But these are rather special circumstances. Another possibility would be to make the rich contribute a higher proportion of the cost of the war in the long run than they could be made to do during the period of hostilities. Keynes had presumably something of the kind in mind when he proposed initially—though not in his later memoranda—that a capital levy should be imposed after the war. But such a levy, by definition, cannot be met from current income and thus a more protracted period would have to elapse before the workers were recompensed. There could, of course, be some intergenerational transfer of the ultimate cost *within* classes.
5. Official thinking on the economics of war went back a long way. In particular, reference should be made to a Treasury memorandum of 1929 on *The Course of Prices in a Great War*. See W. H. Hancock and M. M. Gowing, *British War Economy* (London: HMSO, 1949) pp. 46 *et seq*.
6. As late as 14 August 1939, Keynes observed in a letter to R. F. Kahn 'I shall be most surprised if it ends in war. It seems to me that Hitler's argument is unanswerable that he must get Danzig, because it matters so little to him or to anyone else' (*Collected Writings*, vol. XXII, p. 3). When war came he thought it could be ended soon with a negotiated peace (ibid., p. 37). His failure to anticipate both the length and the intensity of the struggle was reflected in his early suggestions about building up livestock on the farms and about devoting a greater effort to exports. He was, however, by no means alone in making these early under-assessments.
7. *Collected Writings*, vol. XXVII, pp. 29–36.
8. It may also be of interest to add that Lord Cherwell, usually regarded as a monster of black reaction, was on the same side and helped to reassure Churchill. He had come to the conclusion that the extra cost of the Beveridge Scheme over what would be spent on existing schemes would not be an intolerably heavy burden.
9. *Collected Writings*, vol. XXVII, p. 204.
10. See José Harris, *William Beveridge* (Oxford: Oxford University Press, 1978).
11. In the event benefits were raised over the years roughly in line with average pre-tax earnings and were more than doubled in real terms. Thus we have gone far beyond what Beveridge or Keynes anticipated. Yet it is frequently maintained that Beveridge's proposals have not, even now, been accepted. This is a confused complaint that is valid only with regard to the continued use of means test.
12. *Collected Writings*, vol. XXVII, p. 224.

13. Ibid., p. 325.
14. D. Winch, *Economics and Policy* (London: Fontana, 1967) pp. 281–2.
15. Ibid., p. 282.
16. *Collected Writings*, vol. XXVII, p. 267, reprinted from the *Listener*, 2 April 1942.
17. M_2 is used here in Keynes's sense which was not the same as the M_2 of the financial statistics for the United States and some other countries.
18. See D. Robertson, *Banking Policy and the Price Level* (London: P.S. King and Son, 1926)
19. See *General Theory*, pp. 375–6.
20. *Collected Writings*, vol. XXVII, p. 297.
21. Ibid., p. 322.
22. Ibid., p. 328.
23. Ibid., p. 359.
24. Ibid., p. 322.
25. Ibid., pp. 317, 330–1, 365.
26. See J. C. R. Dow, *Management of the British Economy 1945–60* (Cambridge: Cambridge University Press, 1964).
27. *Collected Writings*, vol. XXVII, p. 325 (italics added).
28. Ibid., p. 323.
29. Ibid., p. 319.
30. Ibid., p. 327.
31. Ibid., p. 317–18.
32. See T. W. Hutchison, op. cit., which contains Keynes's articles from *The Times* of 1937, and also comments by Kahn and Hutchison. See also the interesting article by G. C. Peden, 'Keynes, The Treasury and Unemployment', *Oxford Economic Papers* (March 1980).
33. *Collected Writings*, vol. XXVII, p. 335.
34. Ibid., p. 381.
35. Ibid., p. 417.
36. Any attempt to include such a suggestion would, of course, have met with fierce opposition from Labour members of the war-time coalition.
37. *Essays in Persuasion*, p. 341.
38. *Collected Writings*, vol. XXVII, pp. 382–3.
39. Ibid., pp. 385–7.

DISCUSSION

Official Discussant

Professor A. J. Brown: First of all, I'm sure everyone would wish me to thank Professor Wilson for his most perceptive and stimulating paper. It suggests to me two main questions: first, what do we mean, essentially, by a 'Keynesian' policy, and secondly, how does it fit with what Keynes actually advised in practical situations (as opposed to what he wrote on a theoretical level, or what people think he meant by what he wrote)?

The shortest answer to my first question is, surely, contained in the quotation Professor Wilson gave from Keynes's broadcast of 1942. Keynesian policy is policy deliberately intended 'to make sure that there is enough demand to provide employment for everyone' and 'to prevent a demand in excess of the physical possibilities of supply'. In other words, demand management against deflation and inflation; and both of these aspects of demand mnagement have short-run and long-run applications.

So far as short-run policy against deflation is concerned, Professor Wilson has made it clear that Keynes consistently advocated smoothing out the course of public investment, or perhaps using it counter-cyclically. He also thought something might be done to stabilise private investment, but was unspecific about this, partly because, for reasons that I'll come to in a moment, he rejected substantial variation of the long-term interest rate. He was also, as we've just heard, surprisingly shy of unbalancing the current account budget. It may be thought, too, that he was timid in his estimate of the unemployment percentage that constituted 'full employment'. He thought we were approaching it in 1937, but in this connection one should perhaps remember that others did not dismiss this view. Beveridge himself, in 1937 or early 1938, had his research assistant (one Harold Wilson) sitting in Luton Labour Exchange looking for labour-shortages. (I'm afraid I can't remember whether he found any!)

As to the long-run, Keynes's views on the dangers of depression were dominated by the Stagnation Hypothesis—the fear that the world might run out of productive investment opportunities, and the marginal efficiency of capital sink towards zero. That, as Professor Wilson has made clear, was why he rejected the long-term interest rate as a short-term instrument; he was afraid that, if interest was ever high, people would not believe that it would stay low when the need came for it to be low.

So, in the field of anti-depression policy, Keynes was rather a timid Keynesian for the short-run; and for the long-run his views were radical in a way that has since become unfashionable—though my guess is that, if and when we stop worrying about stagflation, the stagnation hypothesis will be well up among our candidates for the next thing to worry about.

What about Keynes's advice on anti-inflation policy? It seems to me that, despite his reputation as the prophet of anti-depression policy, who neglected the danger of inflation, he did, in fact, in *How to Pay for the War* lay down the pattern of short-term policy against demand-inflation for the post-war period. The Post-War Credit scheme for helping to contain wartime inflationary pressure was only a side-issue. Those of us who sat in the Economic Section in the Treasury after the war (of whom several are here today) will remember that the Keynesian concept of the inflationary gap gave us the precise basis for the overall planning of that day, when the instruments of war-time planning (especially manpower control) were disappearing. What is undeniable is that Keynes failed to foresee the *long-term* danger of inflation that would arise in the labour market in spite of the avoidance of inflationary gaps. (One can't, I think, say that no-one foresaw it; Michael Kalecki saw it very clearly.)

It seems, then, that, in all this which Professor Wilson's paper has brought out, there is a not-unpleasing touch of paradox. On the basis, perhaps, of the most famous of all his dicta, Keynes is popularly regarded as the champion of short-term policy, and primarily (inevitably from the circumstances in which his main works were written) of short-term policy against depression. But in his practical advice, he turns out to have been timid about precisely that area—certainly more timid than the young men of the war-time Economic Section. His deepest fears of depression were long-term. He was clear and lastingly influential on short-term demand-management against inflation, though there his advice did not contain the magic ingredient which we now see to be required if wage-levels are to be prevented from running out of control after a long period of full employment. But then, since the required ingredient has also eluded us, at the practical level, we are in no position to throw stones.

General Discussion

Sir Norman Chester: I only want to add a footnote to the point Tom Wilson made about Keynes's influence on Beveridge's report on social insurance. Keynes persuaded Beveridge to distinguish between the immediate post-war years and the longer period. Beveridge intended at first to recommend that his whole scheme of higher pensions and benefits should be brought in immediately. Keynes, however, though optimistic that after the transition the country could stand the finance of the scheme, was worried about the immediate post-war years. He therefore urged Beveridge to bring in his scheme in two stages, considerably reducing the cost in the early years. As a result the scheme was financially quite attractive and viable, so much so that I did not find it difficult to persuade Donald MacDougall and Professor Lindemann (Lord Cherwell) that they could present it favourably to the Prime Minister.

It is true, however, that as regards the longer run there was a big gap between the views of Maynard Keynes and Hubert Henderson as to the likely level of the post-war national income. Henderson was pessimistic, citing war damage, loss of overseas assets and the probability of difficulties for international trade. Keynes took an optimistic view believing, for example, that the war had ended many labour restrictive practices and introduced innovations and new techniques. Their sharply contrasting opinions caused difficulties when ministers and the Treasury came to consider what they might be able to afford after the war.

One of the few triumphs I had with the Treasury was to produce about this time a generally agreed estimate of the likely national income in the first post-war year. It was thought to be neither unduly pessimistic nor unduly optimistic and became the figure on which policy decisions were made.

Lord Balogh: I think that the contributions so far have neglected the fact that there wasn't one Keynes; there were many 'Keyneses'. There was a 'Robertson'

Keynes; there was a 'Joan' Keynes; there was a 'Kahn' Keynes, and in the end there was of course a 'Robbins–Meade' Keynes and this explains a very great many things which seem to bother Professor Wilson, though it didn't bother Lord Kaldor so much. Of course he restricted his analysis to the pre-period when the political problem of planning and control was not quite as clear as later on. This comes out very clearly in my experience with Keynes when at the very beginning of the war I was working in the French Embassy, and thus had access to certain papers which interested Keynes, and I was in close touch with him, and we both worked for the institution of exchange control, which he disliked, but up to that moment was in favour of. He published an article of mine on the import of gold into France (*Economic Journal*, September 1930) and wrote on those lines a memorandum to the Treasury. Now immediately, as he went into the Treasury, his former antipathy against direct controls revived, and I can't imagine that his environment did not have a great influence on him. He really adapted himself very closely to his environment, though he expressed the ideas very much more brilliantly than those who originated them, and who had an impact on his thinking. It seems to me that this aspect of his nature and thinking has not been brought out, and, in a way, of course, ought to be.

Professor Kaldor: On the question of wage-push inflation, sometime in the middle of the war I was unexpectedly rung up by Keynes and invited to dinner and he told me he wanted to have my views on how to deal, in a full employment economy, with cost-push inflation caused by excessive increases in wages. He said, I haven't got an answer to this and I thought you were the only one who might invent one. This was at the time when Joan Robinson had published two articles in *The Times* which bore on this point (I think under the influence of Kalecki's political trade cycle) and Keynes suddenly realised that full employment means a change in the relative bargaining strengths of capital and labour which might lead to a continuous upward push of wages, and he thought very much that this might be a very serious matter, from the point of view of full employment policy. The other point was it's true he wasn't in favour of counter-cyclical fiscal policy very much, but he believed very strongly in what is called a fiscal stabiliser; that is to say that, if there is a recession then the budget goes into deficit with increased expenditures and lower tax revenues; you mustn't do anything about that. I mean his advice to Mrs Thatcher would have been: 'for goodness sake don't do that, it's just poisonous what you're trying to do. You must let the deficit go up because that narrows it and vice versa.' And that I think was an important feature. He was not in favour of year-by-year budget stabilisation by any means. On the contrary, that is clear from his work—even his war time work—on *How to Pay for the War*. He wanted to have a budget so as to prevent both excess demand and inflation. But I quite agree with you, in counter-cyclical measures he would have preferred to rely more on the expenditure side than on the revenue side of the account, and he may have been wrong because the exenditure side was a much less plastic sort of instrument—more difficult to regulate than revenue.

Sir Austin Robinson: May I add words here as to what Keynes was actually doing during the war. I thought Tom Wilson brought out extremely well the watershed in the way the war was run round about 1941 to 1942. Down to there, the budgetary demands were really very important, and his contribution in Kingsley Wood's budget was fundamental. But, as Tom Wilson was saying, thereafter the control of resources was almost entirely conducted by other means, by the manpower allocations, by the raw material allocations, by food rationing, by clothes rationing, by fixing costs of living and trying to prevent in that way a wage inflation. But it still remained rather important to mop up surplus income so that you didn't create black markets. I think that became in the later stages of the war the main function of the budget. Keynes during that period was not only concerned with the post-war world, he was also very much concerned with the external finance of the war. Throughout this period we were depending for food, and raw materials, heavily on Colonial territories, on other parts of the world, and it was Keynes who was looking after the problems of the building up of the foreign balances in London; this was one of the increasing headaches of the post-war world, and Keynes was very much in the centre of all of that.

Professor A. P. Thirlwall: Following on from what Professor Kaldor was saying about wage inflation, Keynes was clearly concerned with this long before the war. In his chapter on the theory of prices in the *General Theory*, where he is attacking the mechanistic quantity theory of money, he gives at least three reasons why prices may rise before the level of full employment is reached. First, he mentions that, since resources are not homogeneous, there will be diminishing returns as employment expands. Secondly, he talks about bottlenecks in particular sectors, and prices rising in these sectors long before overall full employment is reached. Thirdly, the wage unit will tend to rise with the increased bargaining position of trade unions and entrepreneurs will be more ready to meet demands for higher wages if business is buoyant. On the basis of Keynes's pamphlet *How to Pay for the War* there is a tendency to think of the 'Keynesian' explanation of inflation in terms of an inflationary gap, and yet here in chapter 21 of the *General Theory* we have modern cost-push and structural theories of inflation precisely anticipated. I have never understood why there should be difficulty in explaining stagflation within a Keynesian framework.

Session 2

INTRODUCTION

Professor M. J. C. Vile (Chairman)

It is a fact of University life that economists, political scientists and historians tend to be narrow in the approach to their disciplines. This afternoon we recognise that in the real world, economics, politics and history cannot be kept separate. In this second session we have an historian and a political scientist who will approach Keynes as an adviser from a rather different angle. Professor Carr is Professor of History at the University of Sheffield and has written extensively on German history from the early nineteenth century right up to, in a recent book, Hitler. I ask him now to talk on the topic of 'Keynes and the Treaty of Versailles'.

JOHN MAYNARD KEYNES AND THE TREATY OF VERSAILLES[1]

Professor W. Carr

It is a considerable achievement for any individual to write a book which exerts a profound influence in the author's own lifetime. To write two such works guarantees the author a place in *The Guinness Book of Records*. John Maynard Keynes has most certainly earned this distinction on the basis of his best-known publications: *The Economic Consequences of the Peace*, which appeared in 1919, and *The General Theory of Employment, Interest and Money* which appeared seventeen years later.

In my contribution to this 'civilised disagreement', as the Master of Keynes College described a previous seminar, I will be concerned with the former work which established Keynes as a professional writer of outstanding ability. It is my intention to commence with some general observations on the book; secondly, I will examine Keynes's views on reparations against the background of the German situation between 1919 and 1933; thirdly, I will make a few comments on the rise of Nazism; and I will conclude with some analysis of Keynes's opposition to the appeasement policy of the British government in the 1930s.

I trust it will not be thought facetious if I speculate for a few moments on the circumstances in which the *Economic Consequences* appeared. I must confess that I am vastly intrigued by the spectacle of a successful Treasury official of immense ability and impeccable bourgeois origins—Eton and King's—breaking the house rules of the ruling classes and washing their dirty linen in public. You must not take it amiss if, as a biographer of the late A. Hitler who has had perforce to dabble in psychohistory without, I hope, being too deeply infected by it, I look around for a psychological explanation of the phenomenon.

I suggest, tentatively, that the explanation may lie in the nervous breakdown Keynes suffered in the summer of 1919. His exhaustion was occasioned as much by mental anguish as by overwork. His action in joining the war-time Treasury alienated him from his Bloomsbury friends. They taunted him for staying at his post despite the fact that he shared, if not their pacifism—for Keynes was not opposed to war on principle—then at least their dislike of conscription which they regarded as a profoundly illiberal measure. The strain of doing a job he liked and did extremely well conflicted with deep personal loyalties and must have been compounded by disillusionment with the Paris Peace Conference precipitating a serious personal crisis.

Was *The Economic Consequences of the Peace* an act of reparation, an attempt to repair the broken bridges to Bloomsbury? It is interesting that, although Keynes, as a man of liberal convictions, had no sympathy with the power politics of the pre-1914 era, he showed understanding for the polities of Clemenceau, the French premier. 'One could not despise or dislike him', he wrote, 'but only take a different view as to the nature of a civilised man or indulge at least a different hope.'[2] It is Woodrow Wilson whom Keynes attacks, and what he condemns is Wilson's weakness in allowing himself to believe that what he did at Paris was consistent with his principles when it was not. For while Wilson was willing to make concessions to meet the points raised by the allied powers, he insisted that their demands must be reconciled with the various pronouncements he had made in recent months. The result was 'the weaving of that web of sophistry and Jesuitical exegesis that was finally to clothe with insincerity the language and substance of the whole treaty. The word was issued to the witches of all Paris:

> Fair is foul and foul is fair,
> Hover through the fog and filthy air.[3]

Thus, for example, instead of declaring openly that the union of Austria and Germany was prohibited unless France permitted it, the treaty declared that Germany would respect the independence of Austria and that this independence was inalienable unless the Council of the League of Nations decided otherwise—and the relevant clause did not go on to say that such a decision would require unanimity on the part of the Council. In other words, 'the honest and intelligible purpose of French policy, to limit the population of Germany and weaken her economic system, is clothed, for the President's sake, in the august language of freedom and international equality'.[4]

I wonder if Keynes was not nauseated by the shortfall between Wilson's lofty principles and his acquiescence in shabby compromises precisely because of his (Keynes's) own inner conflict during the war? Psychologists might also point to the violence of Keynes's language as evidence of suppressed tension even if he did rationalise his vigorous polemical style later on in the memorable phrase: 'words ought to be a little wild—for they are the assault of thoughts upon the unthinking'.[5] We know, too, that Keynes never drove on dipped headlights; once convinced of the correctness of a position, he defended it ruthlessly, relentlessly and even unscrupulously, so some critics aver. There can, incidentally, be little doubt that his intemperate language and his notorious inability to suffer fools gladly—especially pompous official ones of whom there is never a shortage—explains some of the initial opposition to the book.

However, whatever his motives may have been, there is no doubt that Keynes more than any other man helped to create a climate of opinion in Britain and in other countries highly critical of the Treaty of Versailles. Not that his voice was the only one raised in 1919. It was, after all, General Smuts, the South African premier, a man also greatly disappointed by events in Paris, who at first urged Keynes to write the book (and later tried to dissuade him) at a time when leading Liberal and Labour politicians were also expressing grave reservations about the German treaty. Nevertheless, it was Keynes who put into matchless prose what others were thinking, and earned for himself in later years the (undeserved) title of the spiritual father of appeasement. Looking back sixty years later in a vastly changed world, what thoughts occur to a historian reflecting on the political advice contained in *The Economic Consequences of the Peace*?

Three points strike me. In the first place, it is often said that Keynes's portraits of three of the Big Four, i.e. the American president and the British, French and Italian premiers, who dominated the proceedings at Paris are unfair, especially the brilliant and savage vignettes of Lloyd George and Woodrow Wilson. I do not subscribe to this opinion. After all, these did not purport to be more than thumbnail sketches serving a polemical purpose. As his biographer remarks: 'the sketches give only part of the truth'.[6] Nor should it be forgotten that Keynes omitted a far more uncomplimentary picture of Lloyd George and only published it many years later.[7] And, though Keynes exposed mercilessly what he took to be weaknesses in Wilson, he was generous enough to concede that 'his temperament allowed him to leave Paris a really sincere man; and it is probable that to this day he is genuinely convinced that the Treaty contains practically nothing inconsistent with his former professions'.[8] What I do detect in Keynes is a contempt for the workaday world of the politician whose high principles are constantly modified by the exigencies of office and restrained by the parameters within which policies have to be formulated. For example, according to Keynes, when the Big Four met for their confidential deliberations they 'fulfilled their destinies in empty and arid intrigue'.[9] Or, meeting in public session, Lloyd George and Woodrow Wilson are described by Keynes as being 'the centre of a surging mob and babel of sound, a welter of eager impromptu compromises and counter-compromises, all sound and fury signifying nothing'.[10]

I cannot help feeling that the Earl of Crawford was right when he wrote in his diary in April 1919 that Keynes 'is a wonderful fellow but has passed his life in cloister and has no experience in handling men or assessing temperaments'.[11] The same sentiment was in the mind of the wit who penned those famous lines in *Punch* in 1920:

> There was a superior young person called Keynes
> Who possessed an extensive equipment of brains
> And, being elected a Fellow of King's
> He taught Economics and similar things.
>
> And while we're amused by his caustic dispraise
> Of President Wilson's Chadbandian ways,
> Of the cynical TIGER laconic and grim,
> And our versatile Premier so supple and slim—
> Still we feel as he zealously damns the allies
> For grudging the Germans the means to arise
> That possibly some of the Ultimate Things
> May even be hidden from Fellows of King's.[12]

Surely David Thomson, the late Master of Sidney Sussex College, was nearer the mark when he summed up the work of the peacemakers in these memorable words:

> They were not ... men behaving like gods and reshaping a new heaven on earth. They were tired, harrassed, busy but well-meaning men, groping a way as best they could through the appalling aftermath of war, buoyed up by a hope that if only they could set the train on the track again it might run to a useful destination. The settlement they made ... was the confirmation and acceptance of a new order that was already taking shape around them. That new order was the product of temporary enthusiasms for democratic self-government, of a largely unperceived economic upheaval, and of other results of the war itself. The peacemakers could only trim the edges and try to consolidate.[13]

That appears to me to be a more judicious comment than Keynes's dismissal of the work of the peacemakers as an act that 'outraged Justice, Mercy and Wisdom'.[14] Keynes grossly overestimated the room for manoeuvre at the disposal of the Big Four. It is easy to say with hindsight that

> the fundamental economic problem of a Europe starving and distintegrating before their eyes, was the one question in which it was impossible to arouse the interest of the Four. Reparation was their main excursion into the economic field, and they settled it as a problem of theology, of politics, of electoral chicane, from every point of view except that of the economic future of the states whose destiny they were handling.[15]

Yet as democratically elected politicians the Big Four could scarcely avoid paying some heed to public opinion at home. This is not to deny that Lloyd George shamelessly exploited the situation during the Khaki Election of 1918. But it is a reminder that primitive political passions cannot be disregarded as easily by politicians as by Fellows of King's. Furthermore, as Thomson points out, the Big Four had to accept the reality of a situation hardening out on the ground in 1919/20. New states, fiercely nationalistic in outlook, for whom political independence took precedence over economic viability, were arising phoenix-like from the ashes of the old order and frontiers were coming into existence without reference to the deliberations at Paris. Secondly, I think Keynes also overlooked the plain fact that Germany could have been treated much more savagely. If France had had her way, she would have annexed the Rhineland and the Saarland as a precaution against renewed German aggression. And if the Poles had had their way—and the French encouraged them in their ambitions—Danzig would have become part of Poland. It was thanks to the efforts of Lloyd George and Woodrow Wilson that compromises were arrived at that avoided such gross violations of the principle of self-determination. The Rhineland was demilitarised permanently and was to be occupied by allied troops for fifteen years; the Saarland was placed under the League of Nations until 1935 when a plebiscite returned the area to Germany; and in the case of Danzig a free city was created under a League of Nations commissioner whilst Poland was given certain rights in respect of the commercial life of the port. Similarly over reparations, the fantastic figures being bandied about in allied countries by supposedly responsible financiers in 1918/1919 were not accepted by the Big Four. Instead they set up a Reparations Commission to report in 1921. Although this may have been a mistake in as much as it created uncertainty and discouraged investors whose loans were urgently needed by Germany, the hope was that passions would abate with the passage of time.

However—and this is my third point—Keynes was right on the whole in thinking the allied powers were making a mistake over reparations. The point needs some clarification. For Keynes did not object to reparations in principle. As head of a Treasury team in the autumn of 1918, he was responsible for the report suggesting that Germany could pay a total of £3000 million, though £2000 million was considered a more realistic figure. And when Lloyd George was resisting pressure in the spring of 1919 for a much higher total, Keynes, whatever his private reservations, complied with an instruction to supply arguments in favour of a figure of £5000 millions. What infuriated him was the decision of the allied powers to add war pensions and separation allowances to the total. For this tripled Germany's liability at a stroke, and saddled her with a burden which, in Keynes's opinion, was quite beyond her capacity to pay. To justify a decision hardly compatible with the armistice terms on which Germany had surrendered, the allies inserted in the Peace Treaty the notorious War Guilt clause placing full responsibility for the outbreak of hostilities on Germany. That ill-advised clause symbolised for Germany the humiliation of defeat and simply reinforced her determination to throw off the 'shackles' of Versailles as quickly as possible.

I would remind you of Keynes's reasons for believing that a sum of this size would prove an impossible burden for Germany. As the allies refused to accept German goods—a solution Keynes had favoured, Germany had no option but to pay in foreign exchange;

and Keynes argued that she would be unable to create the enormous trade surplus required to pay so large a sum. Furthermore, if she succeeded in doing so it would be at the expense of British export markets which would make a mockery of her defeat on the field of battle. And behind the cogently argued case lay a gnawing fear that if the allied powers were foolish enough to try and enforce their inflated claims Germany would be impoverished; the economy of Central Europe—which depended on a prosperous Germany—would be disrupted, and the door would be opened for the spread of bolshevism. In Spenglerian mood Keynes saw European civilisation tottering on the brink of disaster in 1919. Only if Germany could be kept in the Western camp by sensible economic policies could a plunge into the abyss be averted.[16]

It is true, of course, that in *A Revision of the Treaty*, published in 1921, Keynes admitted that his first worst fears had not been realised, for two main reasons: first, when it came to it, no serious attempt had been made to enforce the reparations clauses in full; and secondly, the peoples of Europe had been more patient in the face of adversity than Keynes had expected. But he still maintained his basic objection to the size of the reparations demanded of Germany and to the associated problem of the payment of inter-allied war debts. The continuing uncertainties created by these huge burdens were bound in his opinion to have a detrimental effect on the pattern of recovery introducing, as they did, an element of disequilibrium into world trade. And, as a true liberal, he believed that happy and prosperous nations would be peaceful ones; on that premise rested all his hopes for the future.

A word of explanation about war debts. During the war the United States, Britain and France loaned money to the smaller allied powers. By 1922 the United

States was a net creditor for more than $10 000 million and Britain for about $4000 million (she did, of course, owe large sums to the United States), while France was a net debtor. Britain and France favoured cancellation of these inter-allied debts, while Britain (though not France) was also willing to waive her right to reparations as part of a general settlement. Keynes strongly supported Britain in this, believing that, for the time being, France and Belgium should share whatever could be collected from Germany. The American Congress, however, insisted on full repayment of the war debts and refused to recognise the intimate connection between these debts and reparations. In the end the debtors agreed to repay the debts with interest over a period of years. The fact remained, as Keynes pointed out, that the repayment raised precisely the same sort of transfer problem as the payment of reparations and consequently retarded the economic recovery of Europe.

The views of Keynes on the financial and economic unwisdom of the Versailles Treaty were widely accepted in Britain between the wars, although one should remember that men like Winston Churchill, while bowing to Keynes's superior knowledge as an economic expert, were critical of his strictures on other aspects of the settlement. Nevertheless, there was no major attack on Keynes's general thesis until the Second World War when Etienne Mantoux, a French economist and son of the interpreter at the 1919 Peace Conference, published *The Carthaginian Peace, or the Economic Consequences of Mr. Keynes*, a polemical work which appeared in 1946 and attacked Keynes in the same savage language he had used on Lloyd George and Woodrow Wilson.

Basically Mantoux argued that the fact of a second German aggression within twenty-five years was positive proof that Keynes's plea for magnanimity towards Germany in 1919 had been profoundly mistaken and that he bore a heavy responsibility for the misery occasioned by a second war. Furthermore, Mantoux challenged Keynes's view that Germany could not have paid the full amount of reparations. On the contrary, Mantoux argued that Germany did not want to pay reparations whatever the sum involved, and did all she could to avoid paying. And although she was, in fact, saved from having to make real efforts to pay by allied intervention in the shape of the Dawes and Young Plans and by an influx of foreign capital, this considerable easement of her position was rewarded by a second outburst of German aggression in 1939.

Certainly some of the arguments Mantoux employed in his chapter on reparations were patently absurd as Roy Harrod has pointed out.[17] Nor did Mantoux admit that Keynes himself was highly critical of Germany's failure to combat inflation in the early 1920s and to put the country on a sound economic footing. Nevertheless, Mantoux raises issues which are best clarified by examining the German situation in the 1920s and early 1930s in order to determine how significant a factor reparations really were in exacerbating Germany's economic problems.

By the end of the First World War Germany was already experiencing financial difficulties. Like other belligerent lands, she had financed her war effort not through direct taxation but largely through short-term loans and had covered a growing budget deficit by printing money.[18] It was the intention of the Imperial government to make the allies pay for Germany's war. When the moment of truth arrived in 1918, Germany had already accumulated a huge internal debt of 153,000 million marks. The budget deficit continued to rise after the armistice; expenditure escalated because of reconstruction costs, war pensions and debt charges, while inflation eroded the value of higher tax receipts. Then in 1921 a reparations burden of 132,000 million marks was imposed on Germany to be paid over thirty years at an annual rate of 2000 million marks. To cover the ever-widening deficit between receipts and expenditure the government simply printed an increasing volume of paper money. It has been calculated recently, that in terms of real purchasing power, government receipts between 1920 and 1922 were worth only 13,200 million marks whereas expenditure amounted to 33,000 million marks.[19]

Reparations directly affected Germany's balance of payments. Before 1914 Germany, like Britain, was running a deficit on her balance of trade, covering it with interest on foreign loans and the proceeds of banking and shipping. By 1919 the situation had changed dramatically; exports had slumped and investments had dwindled; but, as the German need for imports was greater than ever, the mark, already barely half its pre-war value by 1918, continued to fall steadily.

As I remarked a moment ago, the allied powers refused to accept reparations in the form of goods, so that Germany was obliged to pay this debt in foreign exchange. Up to 1921 she managed to pay the allies' interim demands either in gold and silver or by realising foreign securities. However, when faced with the prospect of finding 2000 million marks a year, she was in real difficulties; for at a time when she was selling marks to purchase the necessary foreign currency, foreign investors were already selling their German investments. The result was to greatly accelerate the fall of the mark; between May and November 1921 the mark fell from 14.8 to the dollar to 62.4 and prices in Germany trebled. The fall in the value of the mark also added to the mounting internal debt because more marks were needed to pay the annuities. The Reparation Commission's decision to reduce the 1922 annuity to 72 million marks and the six-month moratorium on all payments which followed shortly afterwards did not help Germany. The mark fell catastrophically in the second half of 1922; between June and December it fell in relation to the dollar from one-third to one-hundredth of a cent. The end came with hyper-inflation in 1923. When the French and Belgians occupied the Ruhr in January in a desperate attempt to obtain reparations at the point of the bayonet, the German government responded by encouraging passive resistance in the area. To pay the wages and salaries of those on strike the printing presses poured out bank notes. The result of these events was to render the mark virtually worthless; in January the dollar was worth 17,972 marks; by November, it had reached the astronomical level of 4,200,000 million marks.

I conclude from this survey that, although reparations were clearly not the primary cause of Germany's economic troubles, nevertheless they were a major factor in exacerbating these difficulties between 1921 and 1923. Of course, Mantoux is quite right in thinking that the German government did less than one might have expected to put the economy in order. And, as mentioned above, Keynes from his close knowledge of the German situation, was also of this opinion.

Why, then, did the Germans do so little to control inflation? I do not think this was due to wilful neglect on the part of the government. More likely it was paralysed by the enormity of the task, and confused by the pull of conflicting interests. For if the government wanted to win the battle against inflation it would have to impose higher taxation and maintain strict credit control. But could a new democratic government, with a precarious foothold in German society and ringed around by powerful vested interests filled with nostalgia for the old imperial regime, afford to alienate still further small entrepeneurs already indignant about the higher taxes introduced by Finance Minister Erzberger?

There were other compelling reasons for taking no action. Inflation was, in fact, positively advantageous to Germany. As the mark fell in value, Germany's export trade picked up again; unemployment fell sharply from 3.7 million in 1919 to 1.5 million in 1922; and during the industrial boom of 1920–2 the Gross National Product reached 80 per cent of the pre-war level.

Much emphasis is usually laid on the disastrous long-term political effects of the erosion of middle-class savings in this period. That is certainly a factor which cannot be ignored in explaining the disillusionment towards the Republic on the part of an important section of the German people. Even so, we must remember that, while savings were decimated, people with mortgages did benefit substantially from inflation as did the farming community. The great industrial magnates and the working class were also beneficiaries; the real assets of the former appreciated, while full employment is seen by one leading economic historian as extremely important in reconciling the working class to the new republican institutions.[20]

Germany recovered quite quickly from hyperinflation. One of the reasons for the general improvement in her position by 1924 was the Dawes Plan. At the height of the 1923 crisis when the Weimar Republic seemed certain to flounder in a welter of economic chaos and political disorder, the United States government, anxious to protect its investors, and the British government, eager to see its best pre-war customer restored to economic health, pressurised the French into accepting a less rigid policy towards Germany.

This interim settlement of the reparations question did not, it is true, alter the total sum payable. But it did attempt to establish what Germany could reasonably afford to pay. It was decided that in the first year Germany would pay 1000 million marks rising gradually to 2500 million marks by 1928/9 and after that by annuities reflecting the prospertity of the economy. To finance the initial payment and to underwrite the newly established currency Germany received 800 million gold marks. To protect the currency still further an agent general for reparations in Berlin, assisted by an international committee, was empowered to suspend payments if the transfer of foreign exchange was likely to affect the mark adversely. It was specified that the German budget would contribute 1250 million marks towards reparations while the remainder would come out of the interest on mortgages imposed on German railways (11,000 million marks) and industry (5000 million marks). Some restrictions were placed on German sovereignty which rankled for years in the minds of right-wing opponents of the Republic; for example, to prevent the government being tempted to pay reparations by printing more notes (with inflationary consequences), the *Reichsbank* was made an independent institution controlled by a board half of whose members were foreigners. A similar board was set up to control the railways which were taken out of public control. Finally, in order that the wheels of industry might start turning again, the French and Belgians agreed to evacuate their forces from the Ruhr in the near future.[21]

The stabilisation of the situation in Germany was followed by an influx of foreign capital, half of it from the United States. This was of crucial importance for it solved Germany's transfer problem enabling her to pay reparations in the second half of the 1920s. Between 1924 and 1929 Germany borrowed abroad 25,000 million marks of which 10,000 million were re-invested abroad. During roughly the same period Germany paid out 11,000 million marks in reparations.

Finally, in 1929 the Young Plan brought about a further easement of Germany's position. The reparations total was fixed at 112,000 million marks with payments, at approximately 450 million marks below the Dawes rate, continuing until 1987. The irksome controls over the *Reichsbank* and the railways were removed, and Germany was at last made solely responsible for all payments. In the event of difficulties a newly established Bank of International Settlement would decide whether to defer payments.

There is no doubt that Germany made no serious attempt to pay reparations out of taxes and savings in the second half of the 1920s.[22] To attribute this to a wilful decision on the part of the German government to cheat the allied powers would be misleading. The fact was that the economy was already in an unhealthy state during the so-called 'golden twenties'. Despite a veneer of prosperity, 'stagflation' would be a more apt description certainly by the end of the 1920s.[23] Production rose only by fits and starts (e.g. in 1924/5 and 1926/7) falling to a negative growth rate in 1928/9. Unemployment averaged 1,300,000 throughout this period with 3,000,000 out of work in February 1929, just some months before the official onset of the world economic crisis. Germany was also exporting less than in 1914 (owing, as Keynes pointed out in 1929, to higher wage levels). Yet, despite a lower Gross National Product, social expenditure was markedly higher than before 1914 with heavy spending on housing and municipal services. Deficits in the budget and balance of payments were, therefore, a feature of the period as a whole. It would not be unfair to say that Germany masked her failure to get down to the task of paying reparations out of her own resources by allowing herself to become dependent on short-term loans from abroad. It must be said in extenuation that no Weimar government felt strong enough to demand the sacrifices necessary from all classes to correct the imbalance between social expenditure and flagging production. It was easier to blame reparations for the mounting difficulties facing the Republic by 1929.

Under the Bruening Government, which presided over a critical period in the slide from parliamentary democracy to dictatorship between 1930 and 1932, reparations played a central role in the chancellor's strategy. Let me explain that in view of the political deadlock in the Reichstag in the winter of 1929/30, President Hindenburg, at the suggestion of his unofficial advisers, appointed Heinrich Bruening as the first of the so-called presidential chancellors. Though expected to work with the Reichstag as far as possible, Bruening could, if necessary, use the president's powers (under article 48 of the constitution) to promulgate legislation without that body's consent. We know now that Bruening came to power fully determined to free Germany from the disarmament and reparations provisions of the Versailles Treaty. Under him the needs of the economy were ruthlessly subordinated to the search for a foreign political success calculated to appease the rising tide of national feeling at home.

So far as reparations were concerned, Bruening realised that the creditor nations were perfectly happy to see Germany pay reparations indefinitely through the medium of foreign loans because they knew that the alternative was to earn foreign exchange through a favourable balance of trade which would be at their expense. Precisely for this reason Bruening decided to engineer an export drive which, since the Young Plan had removed all foreign controls, could not be prevented by the creditors. Ruthless deflation at home in the shape of wage reductions, price cuts and increased taxation on consumer goods, coupled with support for industry would, he hoped, make German goods more competitive in world markets. At the same time massive financial aid was given to German agriculture and tariffs were raised in order to reduce Germany's dependence on foreign supplies, thus increasing still further the economic difficulties of the creditor nations. Out of the anticipated trading surplus Germany would pay reparations without being dependent any longer on foreign loans. And, as the surplus would have been built up at the expense of the creditors, Bruening hoped that commercial interests in these lands would pressurise their governments to abandon reparations entirely.

Bruening did succeed in this objective. As foreign money poured out of Germany and the economy plunged downwards, President Hoover proposed a one-year moratorium on all reparations and war debts in 1931. When the economic situation showed no sign of improvement a year later, the creditor nations met at the Lausanne Conference in July 1932 and abrogated the Young Plan. In return Germany was required to hand over to the Bank for International Settlement bonds worth 3000 million gold marks as a final payment. But in effect this was the end of reparations. In all Germany probably paid some 37,500 million marks, 26,000 million before the Dawes Plan took effect and 11,000 million between 1924 and 1932. Against this has to be offset 25,000 million marks Germany borrowed abroad in the second half of the 1920s. However, Bruening's foreign political success came too late to save him; in May, President Hindenburg dismissed him from office. And in any case the success had been dearly bought. As export prices were falling all over the world and tariff barriers were going up, Bruening's export drive failed. German unemployment did not fall but rose from 2.3 million in 1930 to 6.0 million in 1932. Meanwhile in the politically sensitive countryside agrarian prices continued to fall. It is significant that from the autumn of 1931 onwards Bruening's most enthusiastic supporters, who were found in industrial and landowning circles, were beginning to desert a man whose deflationary policies had simply exacerbated the crisis, and were looking elsewhere for salvation.

So I come now to the third part of my lecture, and to the major question: was Keynes right when he blamed Hitler on the Versailles Treaty? Professor Cranston speaking at the 1976 Keynes Seminar was of the opinion that 'if what he [Keynes] had recommended at the time of Weimar had been adopted, there is every likelihood that Hitler would never have come to power'.[24] I do not feel as confident as Professor Cranston that this would have been the case and I would like to elaborate on this point.

Let me remind you, first of all, that Hitler's small Nationalist Socialist party remained on the lunatic fringe of German politics between his release from Landsberg prison in 1924 and the 1929 crisis. In other words, as long as Germany enjoyed some semblance of prosperity and gradually regained her old status in Europe (as she did to some extent under the guidance of Stresemann) popular support for extreme right-wing politics was limited.

What turned the Nazis into a mass party with considerable electoral support was not opposition to the Treaty of Versailles but the impact of the world economic crisis on a creaking political system already facing intractable social and economic problems at the close of the 1920s. It was the coincidence of economic and political crisis that opened the way for Hitler to come to power.

Of course, the Nazis beat the nationalist drum harder than the other parties, and made capital out of the 'Versailles dictate' and the 'interest slavery' which they alleged the Dawes and Young Plans had imposed on Germany. But it is indicative of the relatively limited support right-wing extremism enjoyed at the close of the 1920s that a noisy campaign launched in 1929 to promote a law against the 'enslavement of the German people' was a failure. The sponsors of a bill which demanded the immediate repudiation of the War Guilt clause, the suspension of reparations and the indictment of Stresemann for signing the Young Plan attracted only 4,000,000 signatures, just sufficient to oblige the authorities to put the issue to the people in a referendum. It was heavily defeated with only 5.8 million (13.8 per cent of the total electorate) voting in favour.

I do not deny that the treatment of Germany in 1919 was an important variable in the historical equation. But I would draw attention to several other variables: the economic discontents of the middle class and especially of the small farmers who turned increasingly to the Nazis after 1928; a lack of faith in the parliamentary system which was virtually abandoned in the winter of 1929/30 before the full effects of the world crisis were apparent in Germany;[25] fear of communism, a growing political force in the early 1930s; middle-class resentment of working-class gains since 1918; and, last but not least, the action of a group of heavy industrialists and large landowners who pressurised Hindenburg into appointing Hitler Chancellor because Nazi promises to expand the economy by increased state aid (including rearmament) coupled with the destruction of the free trade union movement enabled monopoly capitalism to emerge from the crisis stronger than ever. To sum up on this point: one must accept that German fascism was a socio-economic phenomenon with roots reaching back to the pre-war era, and not the product of a simple gut reaction against the Treaty of Versailles.

Secondly, I would argue that it is a mistake to suppose that the objective of German foreign policy in the 1930s was the revision of the Versailles Treaty; or, to put it another way, to suppose that if Germany had been handled leniently in 1919 she would not have pursued an aggressive policy later on.

It is well known by now that Hitler dreamt of a new German *Reich*, a great racial empire stretching from the Ural mountains to the Atlantic coast. What is not sufficiently appreciated is that the respectable conservatives who supported Hitler (and blamed him when Germany lost the war) were, strictly speaking, not revisionists either. Nor was any Weimar government. The common objective at all times was to make Germany a *Grossmacht*, the dominant power in Central and Eastern Europe, reviving once more the imperialist ambitions of the pre-1914 era.

In pursuit of these ambitions Germany sometimes laid emphasis on the peaceful economic penetration of neighbouring lands. Stresemann, for example, confidently hoped that Germany could dominate the markets of the East and turn communism back into capitalism. It is interesting to note that Keynes himself was very much in favour of German economic activity in the East for the purpose of reviving German markets in Russia and, by so doing, preventing Germany competing with Western countries for the produce of the New World.[26] Bruening, too, had ambitious economic plans which took the form of expansion into the Danubian basin to obtain the cheap raw materials Germany needed for her export drive; the Customs Union with Austria which he proposed in 1931 and which was vetoed by the French, was intended as a first step in this direction reviving dreams of a German-dominated 'Middle Europe', a popular concept during the First World War.

Other Germans, especially in the Foreign Office and army command, thought more in terms of territorial expansion, and their ambitions went far beyond simple revision of the Versailles Treaty. Even the wish for *Anschluss* with Austria was not, strictly speaking, revisionist for Austria was not part of the Reich of 1871 though it had been in the former German Confederation of 1815. Equally, a new partition of Poland, such as Foreign Minister Neurath proposed to Chancellor Hitler at a cabinet meeting in March 1933, went well beyond revisionism. So did the annexation of the Sudetenland and the neutralisation of Czechoslovakia supported by Foreign Office officials and army command in the 1930s. And behind them stood the great monopolistic enterprises whose plans to eliminate competition in Central and Eastern Europe coincided with the territorial ambitions of the Nazis in these areas. Whether the common effort of the conservative Establishment and the Nazi leadership to try and make Germany the dominant power in Europe is a sufficient explanation of German foreign policy in the 1930s, or whether this was but a prelude to Hitler's plans of racial imperialism and world domination, with which many conservatives were not in agreement, is a much larger issue which I cannot discuss in this paper. The point I wish to make here is a more limited one: namely, that while Hitler made great play after 1933 with the 'intolerable burden of the Versailles dictate', the fact is that the treaty system was crumbling away between 1930 and 1933 and was not a major factor in the internal political battles of those years, and that German foreign policy was heavily determined by economic, geographical and strategic realities which preceded that treaty.

Finally, I wish to examine Keynes's reaction to the Hitler phenomenon in the course of the 1930s. You will recall that I said earlier that Keynes is sometimes regarded as the 'spiritual father' of appeasement because his sense of moral outrage at the Treaty of Versailles did much to give a whole generation of liberal-minded Englishmen guilty consciences about the treatment of Germany. Of course, these people were scandalised by Hitler's brutal treatment of political opponents especially the Jews. Nevertheless, they felt it not unreasonable for German-speaking people to come together in one *Reich* if they so wished. The Nazis made great play with the slogan '*Ein Volk, ein Reiche, ein Führer*', and it is no exaggeration to say that they succeeded in turning the flank of the Western powers in the propaganda war by exploiting the nationality principle against them. For the practical question, as it appeared to many Englishmen, was simply whether one could go to war to prevent Germans re-occupying the Rhineland, or German-speaking Austrians joining the *Reich* or three and a half million Germans leaving Czechoslovakia? Many Englishmen thought not.

These sentiments, when combined with the economic, political and strategic realities determining British policy in the 1930s, crystallised out into the policy of appeasement. Regarded in the most favourable light, this was based on the belief that if the grievances of the dictatorships were removed by negotiation around the table, the process would have a therapeutic effect on them and transform them into respectable members of the international community.

At one end of the spectrum appeasement degenerated into pro-fascist and anti-communist sympathies, at the other into a craven desire to avoid war at all costs. This is what some argued had occurred during the Munich crisis when Hitler bullied and blustered at Bad Godesberg, rejecting Chamberlain's proposals, making it perfectly plain that he could not be trusted and had wider designs on Czechoslovakia—nevertheless, Chamberlain and Daladier capitulated to the blackmail.

Was Keynes an appeaser in any sense of the word? That accusation was indignantly repudiated by Professor Cranston. 'If what Keynes recommended after 1933 had been adopted,' he said, 'the excesses of Hitler would have been resisted and thwarted sooner.'[27] Now, I do not disagree with this proposition as a general indication of where Keynes stood on the great issues of that decade, but I would add that his opposition was much more complex and sophisticated than that of many on the Left who saw the situation in terms of a moral choice between surrender to Hitler and resistance to his demands to the point of war, although the very same people opposed rearmament in season and out of season because they refused to trust 'capitalist' governments with guns. In the columns of the *New Statesman and Nation* Keynes castigated this naive and slovenly thinking unmercifully.

As the correspondence between Keynes and Kingsley Martin in the latest volume of the *Collected Writings* demonstrates very clearly, Keynes had no illusions about the Nazis from the earliest days. When Germany withdrew from the Disarmament Conference and from the League of Nations in October 1933 he wrote of the hideous dilemma of allowing Germany 'to call our bluff and arm as and when they choose with what results one can imagine' or of waging preventive war against her.[28]

During the Abyssinian crisis in 1935–6 he was sharply critical of the Foreign Office which he blamed for the failure to enforce sanctions against Italy. He was, incidentally, a strong advocate of sanctions as a weapon against aggressors and pressed for their imposition on Japan when the Sino-Japanese war broke out in July 1937. And in the summer of 1936, although opposed to British involvement in the Spanish Civil War, he came out squarely for rearmament and for a policy of close cooperation between Britain, France, Russia and the United States to hold the 'brigand powers', as he called them, at bay.

Predictably Keynes opposed Chamberlain's policy over Czechoslovakia in 1938. Writing to Kingsley Martin on 1 October he described the Munich Agreement as 'one of the worst pieces of trickery in history'. 'Honourable international policy', he went on, 'has suffered a terrible reverse by the unscrupulous intrigues, quite unsupported by public opinion, of our own pro-Nazis.' He denounced Britain for failing to approach Russia, and Russia for not speaking out clearly. For, although he had doubts all along about Russia's reliability, she had 'played straight into Chamberlain's hands, making it as easy as possible for his policy of ignoring her'.[29] Throughout he expected a sell-out at the expense of the Czechs, and wrote on 8 October that 'neither the Prime Minister nor Herr Hitler ever intended for one moment that the play-acting should devolve into reality. . . . The actual course of events has been dictated by the fact that the objectives of Herr Hitler and Mr. Chamberlain were not different but the same.'[30]

So far so good. But what I find interesting about Keynes's position is that writing to Kingsley Martin at the end of August when the Czech crisis was looming up, he said: 'I agree with you that we should bluff to the hilt; and if the bluff is called back out.'[31] So far as I can judge, Keynes did not say this because he felt that Britain was unable to fight through military weakness, or because of the threatening situation in the Far East which made a peaceful settlement of the Czech dispute highly desirable, or because he knew that the British Dominions were reluctant to go to war for the sake of Czechoslovakia.

I suggest that one can detect three main strands in his mental outlook at this time. In the first place, although Keynes was not a pacifist of the Dick Shepard school, he had a deep and abiding horror of war, partly for moral reasons but partly, I suspect, because he believed, as Karl Marx often did, that war was the catalyst of social revolution; war made no kind of sense to a man who had dedicated his life to propping up capitalism. This strong aversion to war brought him, in practice, very close to Chamberlain's position at the time of the Munich Conference. Secondly, Keynes was strongly of the opinion that things never turn out as one expects in politics. He expressed this most clearly in an article in the *New Statesman and Nation* in July 1937. He wrote:

> It is our duty to prolong peace, hour by hour, day by day, for as long as we can. We do not know what the future will bring, except that it will be quite different from anything we could predict. I have said in another context that it is a disadvantage of the 'long run' that in the long run we are all dead. But I could have said equally well that it is a great advantage of the 'short run' that in the short run we are still alive. Life and history are made up of short runs. If we have peace in the short run that is something. The best we can do is put off disaster, if only in the hope, which is not necessarily a remote one, that some-

> thing will turn up. While there is peace, there is peace. It is silly and presumptuous to say war is inevitable; for no one can possibly know. The only conclusion which is certain is that we cannot avoid war by bringing it on.[32]

'The first duty of foreign policy,' he said later, 'was to avoid war.'[33] This, too, is a sentiment which may, in certain circumstances, predispose one to favour peace at almost any price. The third, and probably the most important, strand was Keynes's belief that, however much one deplored Hitler's methods, the settlement arrived at was a good one. As he wrote to Kingsley Martin on 1 October 1938:

> It is *not certain* that the present settlement may not be a good thing in the long run. Viewed quite drily, there is a good deal to be said for it. . . . The settlement itself cannot rightly be denounced as indefensible and monstrous. What is certain is something rather different—namely that the sympathies and methods which have brought it about cannot safely be allowed to continue in charge. This time they may, by historic luck, have carried through a necessary thing which decent men could not have accomplished. This means that a frontal attack on the settlement itself is not the wisest course.[34]

And again on 4 October he declared: 'The damned thing about the settlement is that from our selfish and short-sighted point of view, there is so much to be said for it. Good *may* result from what no wise or good man could have brought himself to accomplish. Vile and dirty work can be beneficial to those who do it—or do you believe in the eternal justice of the world? I don't.'[35] Not perhaps all that surprising a view, for

Keynes had done much to propagate the view that the Germans had been cheated in 1919 when the principle of self-determination had not been fully implemented.

In all seriousness I would ask a different question: should that principle have been fully implemented in the case of the Czech–German frontier? As Mantoux quite rightly pointed out, several factors have to be taken into account when delineating a frontier: strategic, economic, geographical and historical, as well as linguistic.[36] Strategically the Böhmerwald was an essential frontier for the new state in the West, while the Sudetenland was an integral part of the historical–geographic unit known in history as the Crown Lands of St Wenceslaus. In these circumstances why should three and a half million Czech citizens be transferred to a foreign land because they happened to speak German as well as Czech, when the result would be to weaken the new state and expose it to pressure from a powerful neighbour?

These reflections lead me to what seems a crucial point for a proper understanding of the British government's attitude to the Munich crisis. When the Great Powers went to war in 1914 there was little doubt in the minds of statesmen that the real issue at stake was the preservation of the balance of power in Europe. Sir Edward Grey, British Foreign Secretary, was perfectly well aware that if Britain did not stand by France, she risked isolation in a Europe dominated by Germany. The difficulty facing the government was that power political considerations do not ordinarily move the mass of the population. It was the 'rape' of 'gallant little Belgium', not the German threat to France, that transformed the crisis into a moral crusade rallying the people round the Liberal government and enabling it to declare war on Germany with a clear conscience. In 1938, however, the situation was different in one particular. Once again few were ready to go to war in defence of the balance of power, threatened though it was by Nazi Germany. What was absent this time was a compelling moral reason for war. Owing to the lamentable confusion of moral principle with the nationality principle, many, including Keynes, supposed that right was on the side of the Germans, or that at the very least they must be given the benefit of the doubt.

As we know only too well, good did not result from the Munich Agreement—only further evil. In March 1939 German troops occupied the Czech state, Bohemia was annexed to the *Reich* and a protectorate proclaimed over Slovakia, while Hungarian troops occupied Ruthenia. It is singularly unfortunate that there is a gap in the correspondence with Kingsley Martin in these months for it would be fascinating to know how Keynes reacted to these events which put Europe on the road to war.

What I find most surprising is that on the very eve of war Keynes was supremely confident that the issue of Danzig and the Polish Corridor would not lead to the outbreak of hostilities. 'Hitler's argument that he must get Danzig, because it does not really matter either to him or to anyone else, seems to me unanswerable', he wrote to Kingsley Martin on 14 August 1939. 'In due course, Danzig will be incorporated in the Reich, which will leave the de facto situation substantially what it is.'[37]

I find his complacency about the future baffling, because Keynes knew perfectly well what Hitler's ambitions were. In 1921 in *A Revision of the Treaty* he declared his belief that when Germany recovered her strength she would look eastwards where 'her hopes and ambitions' lay.[38] And as late as October 1938 he wrote to Kingsley Martin: 'Herr Hitler has explained that his ultimate objective is the Ukraine. The Balkans, Western Europe, the colonies might have been the desired sphere of his expansion. But he has openly decided otherwise; and in these matters he is a man of his word.' Commenting on the Munich crisis, he remarked perceptively that Czechoslovakia in alliance with Russia represented a threat to Hitler's flank, and that he had been obliged for this reason to deal with it first. The next step, he predicted, would be an alliance with Poland 'with a view to the seizure of the Ukraine'.[39] And, indeed, Hitler did negotiate with Poland in the winter of 1938/9, though whether as a prelude to an attack on Russia or to protect his flank for an attack in the West remains an open question.

However, in conclusion it must be remembered that, totally wrong though Keynes, like many others, had been about the likely outcome of the Danzig crisis, once Britain was committed to war his mood of complacency disappeared. There was no moral dilemma for him this time as there had been a quarter of a century before. He stood wholeheartedly behind the government and would have no truck whatsoever with those who still thought in terms of a compromise arrangement with Hitler even after the defeat of Poland.

NOTES

1. Some of the points made in discussion at the seminar have been heeded in this final version of the paper.
2. *The Collected Writings of John Maynard Keynes*, vol. II, *The Economic Consequences of the Peace* (London: Macmillan, 1971) p. 18.
3. Ibid., p. 32.
4. Ibid., p. 33.
5. 'National Self-Sufficiency', pt 5, *New Statesman and Nation*, 15 July 1933; reproduced in *Collected Writings*, vol. XXI.
6. R. F. Harrod, *The Life of John Maynard Keynes* (London: Macmillan, 1957) p. 260.
7. In this essay Keynes described Lloyd George as 'this extraordinary figure of our time, this syren, this goat-footed bard, this half-human visitor to our age

from the hag-ridden magic and enchanted woods of Celtic antiquity. One catches in his company the flavour of final purposelessness, inner irresponsibility, existence outside or away from our Saxon good and evil, mixed with cunning, remorselessness, love of power that lend fascination, enthralment, and terror to the fair-seeming magicians of North European folklore', *Collected Writings*, vol. x, *Essays in Biography*, p. 23.

8. *Collected Writings*, vol. II, p. 33.
9. Ibid., p. 4.
10. Ibid., p. 20.
11. M. Keynes (ed.), *Essays on John Maynard Keynes* (Cambridge: Cambridge University Press, 1975) p. 25; cf. Alwyn Parker, British Establishment officer in Paris, who wrote in his diary of Keynes: 'in politics his illustrations are seldom closely related to logic. That is because he has as little aptitude or taste for politics as you and I have for the refinements of economic speculation'—R. F. Harrod, op. cit., p. 239.
12. *Punch*, 14 January 1920.
13. D. Thomson, *Europe since Napoleon* (London: Longman, 1957) p. 573.
14. *Collected Writings*, vol. III, *A Revision of the Treaty*, p. 168.
15. *Collected Writings*, vol. II, p. 143.
16. In September 1922 Keynes again declared that Europe had need of Weimar Germany as part of its 'joint defence against the dark forces'—*Collected Writings*, vol. XVIII, *Activities 1922–1932, The End of Reparations*, p. 43.
17. R. F. Harrod, op. cit., pp. 276–8.
18. It should be emphasised that this was a general and not a specifically German phenomenon; at the end of 1918 the issue of paper money in Germany amounted to five times the 1914 total, in France to just under four times and in Britain to four-and-a-half times.
19. D. Petzina, *Die deutsche Wirtschaft in der Zwischenkriegszeit* (Wiesbaden, 1977) p. 83.
20. Ibid.
21. Keynes was critical of the plan which he considered unworkable because, (i) the sums involved were too large for Germany's capacity to pay, and (ii) the irksome foreign controls would unite the Germans against it—*Collected Writings*, vol. XVIII, and *The Nation and Athenaeum* (4 October 1924) pp. 254–61. On both counts he was subsequently proved wrong.
22. Keynes was well aware of Germany's failure to control public expenditure and improve her export performance, e.g. his article in *The Nation and Athenaeum* (July 1927) in *Collected Writings*, vol. XVIII, pp. 282–7. Cf. Fisher interview, March 1929, pp. 313–78.
23. K. Borchart, 'Wirtschaftliche Ursachen des Scheiterns der Weimarer Republik' in K. D. Erdmann and H. Schulze (eds), *Weimar Selbstpreisgabe einer Demokratie* (Düsseldorf, 1980) p. 225.
24. A. P. Thirlwall (ed.), *Keynes and Laissez-Faire: The Third Keynes Seminar held at the University of Kent at Canterbury, 1976* (London: Macmillan, 1978) p. 109; cf. R. Harrod, op. cit., p. 273.
25. A leading German authority recently argued that the Weimar Republic

really collapsed in the winter of 1929/30 because of unresolved social and economic problems at a time when the psychological effects of the Versailles Treaty were less in evidence than at any time since 1919. A. Hillgruber, 'Unter dem Schatten von Versailles—Die aussenpolitischen Belastung, der Weimarer Republik: Realität und Perzeption bei den Deutschen', in K. D. Erdmann and H. Schulze (eds), op. cit., pp. 63, 67.
26. *Collected Writings*, vol. II, pp. 186–7.
27. A. P. Thirlwall (ed.), op. cit., p. 109.
28. *Collected Writings*, vol. XXVIII, *Social Political and Literary Writings*, ch. 1: 'Keynes and Kingsley Martin', p. 23.
29. Ibid., p. 139.
30. Ibid., p. 142.
31. Ibid., p. 132.
32. Ibid., p. 69.
33. Ibid., p. 70; cf. pp. 55, 136.
34. Ibid., pp. 139–40.
35. Ibid., p. 141.
36. E. Mantoux, *The Carthaginian Peace* (Paris, 1946) pp. 37–43.
37. Ibid., p. 148.
38. *Collected Writings*, vol. III, p. 128.
39. *Collected Writings*, vol. XXVIII, ch. 1, p. 143.

DISCUSSION

Official Discussant

Professor Robert Skidelsky: My comment will follow Professor Carr's division of his paper into three parts, and discuss briefly his remarks on the origins of *The Economic Consequences of the Peace*, the issues raised by Etienne Mantoux, and Keynes's attitude to Germany in the 1930s.

On the first point, I am sympathetic to Professor Carr's notion of the *Economic Consequences* as an 'act of reparation, an attempt to repair the broken bridges to Bloomsbury'. The critical attitude of Bloomsbury to Keynes's war work is well brought out in a letter to Keynes from David Garnett dated 1915:

> What are you? Only an intelligence that they need in their extremity.... A genie taken incautiously out of King's—taken out of a bottle by savages to serve them faithfully for their savage ends, and then—back you go into the bottle.... You pull the strings and the idol Juggernaut opens its mouth and shuts its eyes.

When the *Economic Consequences* appeared, Garnett wrote 'he had come back to us'. So Professor Carr is quite right as far as he goes. But Keynes's opposition to the Versailles Treaty has to be set in the broader context of the First World War itself.

It is clear that as the war went on, Keynes increasingly loathed and detested Lloyd George: a feeling which was reciprocated. Thus Keynes wrote to his mother in 1917: 'I was approved and included in the final list to get a C.B. this honours list. But when Lloyd George saw it he took his pen and struck my name out—an unheard of proceeding.' Early in 1918, Keynes described Lloyd George's conduct in a letter home as 'an extraordinary compound of humbug, chicane and straightforward lying'. And on 14 April 1918 he wrote: 'Still and even more confidently I attribute our misfortunes to George. We are governed by a crook and the results are natural.'

Partly this dislike of Lloyd George was a counterpart to Keynes's personal friendship with the Asquiths. Keynes was part of the Asquith set, usefully supplementing his Treasury salary by large bridge winnings during agreeable weekends at the Wharf.

But more fundamentally Keynes's dislike of Lloyd George arose out of a basic disagreement about the kind of war Britain should be fighting. Keynes was not convinced that the war needed to go on at all—at least after 1916. But if it were to continue, what sort of a war should it be? Should it or should it not be fought without regard to the state of the foreign balance? Lloyd George wanted to run the war without regard to financial constraints. On the other side, the Asquithians saw in the external constraint a way of limiting Britain's commitment to the war, and thus the destruction of peace-time values. This was the Treasury view. Keynes not only completely identified with it, but armed Asquith's Chancellor of the Exchequer, Reginald McKenna, with his most formidable arguments against Lloyd George's 'great gun' programme; something of which Lloyd George was fully aware.

Essentially Keynes wanted Britain to fight a war of subsidies in the old British tradition; Lloyd George a war of great armies. Keynes wanted Britain to provide the money, and the Allies to provide the armies. Britain tried to do both, and when the money ran out, it was only saved by the United States coming in. The personal note in *The Economic Consequences of the Peace* becomes more understandable in the light of these earlier disagreements.

I have no time to go into the difficult technical question of whether Germany could have paid reparations—a problem much debated between Keynes, Bertil Ohlin and Jacques Rueff in the late 1920s. I just want to touch on the issues raised by Mantoux's criticism of Keynes. The important point is that this was not primarily a debate about economics at all, but argument between the 'economic' and the 'political' approaches to international affairs. Mantoux's chief complaint was precisely that Keynes rested his hopes of peace on purely economic arrangements, ignoring frontiers, sovereignties, and balance of power considerations, and the passions and calculations which these aroused.

And I think there is a good deal in this. There is a strange inconsistency running through Keynes's argument. His case was that had the allies made an *economically wise* peace they would not have to guard so much against German militarism by political measures, as the French wanted. Indeed, in the famous first chapter of his book, he gave an idyllic sketch of a pre-war world unified by economic arrangements. But if the world was really so economically harmonious before 1914, why was there a war at all? On Keynes's own premises it could not have broken out for economic reasons. And if the war had started for political and not economic reasons, why should an economically *sensible* peace stop Germany from trying again? Churchill's criticism, echoed by Mantoux, that Keynes simply ignored the political requirements of a durable peace has much force.

I have little to add to Professor Carr's excellent discussion of Keynes's fluctuating attitude to foreign policy in the 1930s. He hated war, and was always too optimistic about the chances of avoiding it. Like Lloyd George, with whom he now agreed, he tended to see foreign affairs in the 1930s as a diversion from the primary goal of restoring economic prosperity. So once more, as in 1919, he tried to conjure away the political factor. The paradox was that it was the Second World War which vindicated Keynesian economics.

One footnote is worth adding. The thread which runs through the three episodes discussed by Professor Carr is Keynes's generally sympathetic attitude towards Germany. It would be fair to describe Keynes, on balance, as anti-French and pro-German. There was a strong family connection with Germany, and this, I think, exercised a pervasive, if largely unconscious, influence on his attitudes throughout his life.

General Discussion

Dr D. Southern: Three quick points: first, Keynes's objection to the reparation settlement was not to the idea of reparations as such. It was he, after all, who produced the figure that £2000 million was the limit of Germany's capacity to pay. What he objected to was the addition of Allied war-pensions to the reparations bill, which had the effect of tripling the overall bill and raising it to what he regarded as a fantastic figure, and also necessitated the War Guilt clause in the Versailles Treaty. Secondly, it wasn't so much that Keynes wanted an economic settlement as that he believed that prosperity was more likely to make nations peaceful than penury, and he always linked his denunciations of Versailles with denunciations of the settlement of inter-Allied debts because he believed that these two *together* would prevent prosperity being restored to the post-war world. Thirdly, Keynes did appreciate that German governments weren't doing as much as they could to pay reparations because when he went to Germany in the early 1920s to advise the German government on how to stop the inflation, he came to the conclusion that German governments were not sufficiently committed to stopping it.

Professor Kaldor: I was very interested in Professor Carr's lecture, and I must say I find myself in agreement with most of it. I would just like to add a few things, where I disagree with him, concerning Germany. I think the Germans never wanted to pay any reparations. They used reparations as a tremendous bugbear in order to crystallise the feeling of *revanche* and nationalism. I remember when I was in Germany as a young student, I read a book by Maximilian Harden, who was a famous publicist of Wilhelm's days and who published a book in 1926 called *Deutschland, Frankreich, England* in which he contrasted the French attitude to reparations in 1871 (the French did everything to pay the five billion gold marks reparations as quickly as possible) with the German attitude which was to postpone any payment (and, in the end, they only paid to the extent to which this was offset by the inflow of American loans). Now, how big a part Keynes played in this nationalistic anti-reparation sentiment, and in making reparations the centre piece on which German revanchism and nationalism were built, I don't know. I don't think it played a very big part. But Keynes was certainly used for that purpose.

The second point I wanted to make was that you spoke rather favourably of Dr Heinrich Bruening, but I am convinced that Dr Bruening is far more responsible than anyone else for Hitler, and therefore for the Second World War. It was Bruening who, contrary to the constant advice of his Minister of Economics (Professor H. Warmbold), prevented anything being done by way of public works, or wage subsidies that were urged on him, in order to diminish mounting unemployment which reached seven million (not six million) by the summer of 1932, when he was dismissed. And when people came to him and said that the whole German economy will collapse he said: 'I'm not going to allow myself to be deflected when I am only a hundred yards from the goal post.' (He sounds awfully like Mrs Thatcher.) The goal post in that case wasn't the reduction of inflation, it was the final liquidation of reparations. The Lausanne Conference only produced a moratorium, and he thought by demonstrating to the world that Germany will collapse economically on account of reparations, and demonstrating to the world that the whole world is in a state of economic crisis *because* of the German crisis, that he could finally get rid of reparations this way. Actually he was dismissed in May. The ideas of the Minister of Economics which he refused to countenance, for reasons that he was only a hundred yards from the goal post and he mustn't change horses, were reversed by his successor, von Papen, who came into power at the end of May 1932. When the Minister of Economics presented him with his plans, he said: 'I don't understand any economics, but if you tell me that Bruening was dead against it, then go ahead—it must be something good.' The Papen Plan was fairly speedily adopted; it reversed the whole German economic situation; unemployment fell by 200,000 for the first time in the month of September

1932; it fell again very substantially in October, and when elections came in November the Nazi vote was diminished by 2 millions as compared to the elections of June 1932. So when Hitler came into power as a result of a series of intrigues and coups, through Schleicher and Hindenburg, not constitutionally, whereas his intention had been to wait till he got the Parliamentary majority, that was because he knew his days were numbered because the tide turned. Well, if Bruening had done a year earlier what Papen did, Hitler could never have made the coup and the whole thing would not have happened.

Dr A. Smith: I think it should be stressed that Keynes was by no means alone in being anti-French and that those liberal and socialist intellectuals who applauded *The Economic Consequences of the Peace* so enthusiastically in 1919 were motivated as much by their fear and hostility towards France—a hostility that for former radicals dated back to a pre-war tradition of dissent over foreign policy—as by their feelings that Germany had been hard done by by the Versailles Conference; in fact, if you look at Keynes's own paper in the 1920s, the *Nation*, time and again it joins the *New Statesman* in expressing this suspicion of 'French hegemony'. In other words, there was very little sympathy for continued French complaints about the absence of any credible Anglo-American guarantee of their security. Clearly, I am not suggesting that one should divorce the problem of French security from the central problem of reparations, but I think it is important to acknowledge this very genuine suspicion of an aggrieved ally intent on securing a full settlement from the young German republic.

Professor W. Carr: One or two brief and rather disconnected comments on the discussion. May I say, first of all, how very pleased I am that a mere historian has been so well received by the economic *mafiosi*? This is most gratifying for an outsider like myself. I would like to thank Professor Skidelsky for his kind remarks about my paper. Naturally, I am pleased to hear that he is favourably disposed towards my excursion into the psychology of Keynes and I was interested in the reference to David Garnett. I take the point about Mantoux's book. I was referring specifically to his comments on reparations in chapter 5 of the book. But I readily agree that when one considers the matter in a broader context, there is a fundamental difference of approach between Keynes and Mantoux in their approach to the problem of peacemaking. Keynes was very much in the liberal tradition in emphasising the necessity of getting the economic relationships between nations right in the hope that power-political conflicts would be thereby diminished. Mantoux, on the other hand, did not think the lion and the lamb could ever lie down together. Like his fellow countryman, that old *Realpolitiker* Clemenceau who thought there were 'seventy million Germans too many', Mantoux believed that the Germans were a naturally aggressive people and that the Versailles Treaty—which he considered fair and reasonable—ought to have been enforced to keep them in order.

Turning to Dr Southern's comments, I agree with him that Keynes did not object to reparations on principle but only to the addition of pensions and allowances. Clearly I conveyed an erroneous impression in my paper. Similarly, with reference to war debts, had time permitted, I should have pointed out that Keynes objected just as strongly to these as to reparations and was concerned primarily about their combined effect on the pattern of recovery. That applies also to the last point Dr Southern made about Keynes's awareness that German governments were not doing all they could to pay reparations; that was true in the early 1920s when he criticised the failure to restrict public expenditure. I am pleased that Dr Southern has drawn attention to all these points for it illustrates very clearly the danger of distorting the picture when one tries to compress a large subject into forty minutes. Finally, Professor Kaldor: again, I have given an erroneous impression, this time about Bruening. I don't care much for the policies he pursued with such disastrous consequences for Germany. Indeed, I do not happen to think that German or English Maggie Thatchers are correct either in their diagnosis of economic problems or in their prescriptions for the economy. If I implied any degree of confidence in Bruening's policy that was quite contrary to my intention of simply describing what these policies were. Clearly, a reduction of public expenditure coupled with higher taxation to reduce private spending were not likely to correct the imbalance between production and demand. And by subordinating the needs of the economy to the foreign political goal of ending reparations Bruening obviously deepened the crisis still further. I agree also that Bruening's well-known remark that he had been dismissed when 'a few hundred meters from the goal' was a gross exaggeration. The damage done to the economy by the summer of 1932 could not possibly have been corrected by the modest work-creation programme of 135 million marks which he intended to introduce and which in any case would have run in series parallel to further deflationary cuts in state expenditure. Germany started to move out of the depth of the depression in the summer of 1932 despite, not because of, Bruening's policies, and with the help of the reflationary measures of Papen and Schleicher, modest though these measures were.

However, whether Hitler would have failed to come to power had Bruening done a year earlier what Papen did is another matter. Here I think Professor Kaldor is far too optimistic. The trouble was that Papen lacked credibility in the mind of the public whereas Hitler, as the leader of the largest party, did have credibility for millions of Germans. It was the combination of his electoral power with interventionist economic policies which convinced the men in the corridors of power that the Nazis must be brought into the government. The paradox was that President Hindenburg, by appointing Hitler chancellor, could claim to be acting more democratically than at any time since March 1930 in as much as Hitler was more likely than any of the presidial chancellors to obtain majority support in the Reichstag. That Hitler had no intention of sharing power with anyone was not apparent to the president's advisers in January 1933.

KEYNES AND REPARATIONS*[1]

Lord Balogh

There has been a marked revival of interest in the post First World War German reparation question mainly as a result of the accumulation of short-term balances due to the non-requitable and unrequited oil surpluses. The approach which has been adopted (including the article included in this volume) represents one more aspect of the slippage into pre-1932/34 economics. The problem of 'collection' (*Aufbringung*) becomes the central problem. The outcome is determined by, (a) the elasticity of demand and supply in the receiving and paying countries respectively, and (b) the assumption of the maintenance in the system as a whole of the incomes (and demand) with a shift from the paying to the receiving country. In as much as the problem of 'paying' for the oil surpluses has close affinity with the German reparations problem a second look seems important. There is a grave danger that in seriatim efforts to eliminate the deficits the oil-consuming countries will propel the world economy onto a downward spiral with vast losses of production and welfare—achieving nothing.

When Keynes wrote *The Economic Consequences of the Peace* he had not realised the importance of effective demand, and he was still in the same situation in 1929 in his debate with Rueff and Ohlin.[2] The consequences of this were threefold.

First, the analysis of Keynes and his critics was deficient. Not only did they not consider adequately the

* An invited contribution.

position of the recipient country, but also they contrasted the sum total of reparations imposed with current national income (and Keynes in his original essay with pre-war voluntary saving). This was irrelevant. Germany regained her pre-war national income by 1927 and her recuperative power was then, as it has been since 1948, extremely high. In other words, if aggregate demand had been planned appropriately, reparations could have been made out of a *rising* German national income.[3] This would naturally have minimised the 'collection' problem in the sense of hardship.

Secondly, in analysing the development of the international economy after 1919, both Keynes and Ohlin compounded the analytical confusion by mistaking inadequate effective demand for lower price elasticities of demand.[4] In reality it was the general deflation after the First World War and again after 1929 that made the transfer from the Germans impossible.[5]

Thirdly, and most seriously, by the 1940s Keynes's reputation was such that almost no-one[6] questioned his original analysis of reparations—even though his reputation was founded on views quite inconsistent with the earlier analysis. Indeed many people in Britain thought the 1929 crash and the rise of Hitler were proof of the correctness of Keynes's *original* arguments! That Keynes was right but for the wrong reasons was too subtle a point for most people. As a result, at the end of the Second World War it was widely believed that reparations from current production would necessarily lead to the disorganisation of the world economy and unemployment. These beliefs were the main reason why Britain backed the proposals to extract reparations from Germany purely by dismantling.[7] This in effect would have resulted in 'pastoralising' Germany—and it should have been clear to all experts that this would be unacceptable to the United States and United Kingdom public even if the Cold War had not begun. (Even more fatuous from the British viewpoint was the failure to secure a German contribution for the upkeep of the British Army on the Rhine when the German Federal Republic was granted sovereignty.)

Of course, as we are now only too well aware, no such thing happened and German productive capacity expanded extremely rapidly. It would therefore have been possible, if consumption had been maintained at a slower rate of increase than production, to permit both the reparation payments *and* an increase in investment. Admittedly there is a dilemma here for the victors. They will want to obtain payments but at the same time they will fear that the ex-enemy may recover faster than themselves. However, a judicious compromise would have been possible by stipulating an initial pause or very low level of reparations increasing with the progress of reconstruction so that the transfer would have aided the victor without destroying the ability of the ex-enemy to make the transfer. It is part of the explanation of Britain's post-war decline that his policy was not used.

In spite of the obvious relevance of this explanation, the rise of monetarism and the execration of Keynes (to which we referred above) have been used to obfuscate the issue. As a result, just as in the 1920s, unemployment becomes no longer the result of demand deficiency but is seen as 'structural' or as the consequence of too high a real wage—in either case the question of the level of aggregate demand conveniently disappears from view.

The large industrial countries, just fractionally more sophisticated or more cynical than in the 1930s, have attempted to export unemployment to each other via competitive industrial policies. Moreover, many of these policies have entailed keeping supply higher than it otherwise would have been, while at the same time leaving aggregate demand relatively unaltered in the short run.[8] The result of such disequilibrium has been a further increase in the intensity of competition, and thus probably further reductions in planned investment.

Paradoxically, the failure to *plan* for a *slow* transfer of resources which is the root cause of the present slow growth and high unemployment may have reintroduced the importance of the 'collection' issue. Nobody would suggest that the industrialised countries of the 1970s are incapable in some physical sense of giving up resources—they are all well above any absolute level of poverty. Nevertheless, people have clearly come to expect their present standard of living not only to continue but also to improve, and the failure in recent years of actual economic performance to live up to these expectations has almost certainly contributed to present social tensions and to cost inflation. In other words people have reacted against the attempt to 'collect' goods from them, and the fact that they have been right to do so (because the goods could not be accepted) will not make it any easier to carry out the transfer when the real demands of the desert Arab countries actually occur.

Once the need for cooperative dealing with this problem has been realised, it is clear that a large part of the desert Arab surplus ought to be internationalised through the IMF and distributed according to some sensible principle among the potential 'paying countries'—that is, an agreement should be arrived at between OECD and OPEC on where to deposit and how to use the oil balances. The oil balances could then be kept in a separate Fund: possibly to be lent to Third

World countries. In the absence of a rational solution the money balances resulting from the deficit will be kicked about from one unfortunate country to another with the danger of the whole system going down in a spiral. The fact that in 1978/9 the United States has been constantly exhorted to tighten its monetary policy in order to correct its balance of payments, and that it is now doing so, only confirms our fears—if the materially strongest country in the world has to get rid of its deficit, what hope is there for the weaker countries? Moreover, the present private recycling is becoming increasingly risky as the cases of Zaire and Iran show.[9] There is a real danger at present that we shall not learn the lessons of the past and that we shall follow the path of the 1929–33 catastrophe.

NOTES

1. The present paper is based on an essay by Andrew Graham and myself on 'The Transfer Problem Revisited', *Oxford Bulletin of Economics and Statistics*, vol. 41, no. 3 (August 1979).
2. J. Rueff, 'Mr. Keynes' Views on the Transfer Problem: I. A Criticism', *Economic Journal* (September 1929) pp. 388–99; and B. Ohlin, 'The Reparation Problem: A Discussion: I. Transfer Difficulties Real and Imagined', *Economic Journal* (June 1929) pp. 172–8, and 'Mr Keynes' Views on the Transfer Problem: II. A Rejoinder', *Economic Journal* (September 1929) pp. 400–4.
3. Keynes got close to seeing this in 1919 when he said 'If the Allies were to "nurse" the trade and industry of Germany for a period of five or ten years ... building up markets for her ... a substantially larger sum could probably be extracted thereafter; for Germany is capable of very great productivity.' Unfortunately he immediately preceded this remark by saying that it did not affect his argument for immediate practical purposes. See J. M. Keynes, *Essays in Persuasion* (London: Macmillan, 1972) p. 10.
4. See again their debate in the *Economic Journal* (1929).
5. We are *not*, of course, claiming that this deflation all resulted from the reparation payments but that policy proposals *must* be analysed in the context of what is actually happening in the world.
6. The only exception of which I am aware is my own analysis of this problem in a memorandum to the Editor of *The Times* in August 1945 fearing that the British government would consent to the policy of reparations through dis-

mantling only and stressed the all-importance of the global policies adopted by the recipient. The memorandum was published in Thomas Balogh, *Unequal Partners*, vol. II (Oxford: Basil Blackwell, 1963) pp. 127–39.

7. Keynes himself, according to Moggridge (D. E. Moggridge, *Keynes* [London: Fontana, 1976] pp. 144–6), seems to have been alert to the problem in 1942 but did not take an active interest when Allied discussion went wrong mainly as the result of the pastoralisation proposals of Harry Dexter White, that very inscrutable individual whose stupidity and malice did such damage to the non-communist world. Keynes, even then, did not consider the mechanism of expansion in the 'creditor' countries which would have allowed the transfer without the consequential exports of the 'debtor' bringing ruin to the formers' industries. In the end, the pre-war Keynesian analysis, in a distorted way, led to a total loss of reparations.
8. The only exception to this would be if successive doses of aid to industry represented a significant *net* addition to the budget deficit and if the production that was sustained caused other firms to be more optimistic than they would otherwise have been.
9. Cf. T. Balogh, 'The Limitations of the Safety Net', *The Banker* (1977).

INTRODUCTION

Professor M. J. C. Vile (Chairman)

The last of the papers to be given today is by Sir Norman Chester. Sir Norman has spent most of his life working and studying in the area which we are discussing today. He has written many books on administration and at the present time he is going through the proofs of the first volume of an administrative history of the British government. During most of the war he was a member of the Economic Section of the Cabinet Secretariat, and has considerable expertise, both as an academic and as a practitioner, in the role of advisers in government. I now invite him to give his reflections on the history and role of economic advisers in government.

THE ROLE OF ECONOMIC ADVISERS IN GOVERNMENT

Sir Norman Chester

The title I have been given implies a distinction between those who advise and those who decide. This is, of course, the basic conception of British government. In constitutional theory it is ministers who decide and who are publicly answerable for all decisions taken. The whole of the rest, the Civil Service, are there to carry out the decisions of their political masters. I have assumed that I have not been asked to give just another lecture on the relations between ministers and civil servants in general, but to concentrate on the role of those who give economic advice.

I

Before 1870 or so it was well accepted that to operate successfully a minister needed to have the power to make the top appointments and to fill the vacancies in his department. Even most Permanent Secretaries were appointed from outside. The permanent heads of the Treasury for the 30 years 1840–70 (Sir Charles Trevelyan and Alexander Hamilton) were both appointed from outside the Civil Service. The trend for the next hundred years was to convert every post into a permanent career appointment except for the ministerial head of the department and his Parliamentary Secretary. The new system hinged on the requirement that pensionable appointments could be made only with the certificate of the Civil Service Commission. Any attempt by a minister to appoint somebody to his department without such a certificate roused political and press criticism. He was accused of political jobbery. The implication was that, however different their political views, ministers could be advised by the same career civil servants.

Probably because it undertook new functions outside the normal range of governmental activity the Board of Trade was an occasional exception to this trend. In 1893, for example, Hubert Llewellyn Smith was appointed at the age of 29 as the first Commissioner of Labour in the Board of Trade. He was an Oxford University Extension lecturer, had lived at Toynbee Hall and three years earlier had, with Vaughan Nash, published *The Story of the Dockers' Strike*. He became Permanent Secretary in 1907. In 1908 W. H. Beveridge was recruited, temporarily at first, by the Board of Trade to establish the new system of labour exchanges.

The war of 1914–18 led to the recruitment, on a temporary basis, of a large number of outsiders to operate the various controls and rationing schemes and to manage the production of arms and equipment. At that time there were very few professional economists in the universities. A handful were recruited but primarily for administrative work, e.g. Sydney Chapman, Professor of Political Economy at Manchester, at the Board of Trade. Keynes joined the Treasury in 1915 and became head of the department dealing with external finance and, in 1919, the principal Treasury representative at the Peace Conference. But he had passed second in the Civil Service examination of 1906 and had then served for two years in the India Office.

Once the war was over the temporaries disappeared or, like Sydney Chapman who was made Permanent Secretary to the Board of Trade in 1919, were made permanent with the approval of the Civil Service Commission. Whitehall reverted to the basic conception of a permanent service, entrance to which was tightly controlled by the Civil Service Commission, with advice reaching ministers through a career, politically-neutral, Administrative Class.

The Haldane Committee which examined the machinery of government in 1917–18 came to the conclusion that 'in the sphere of civil government the duty of investigation and thought, as preliminary to action, might with great advantage be more definitely recognised'. They urged that all departments should make better provision for enquiry, research and reflection before policy was defined and put into operation. For some purposes the necessary research should be carried out or supervised by a department specially charged with the duty but working in the closest collaboration with the administrative departments. Special attention should be paid to the method of recruiting those employed on such work. Later in their report they stressed the need of departments to avail themselves of the advice and assistance of advisory bodies so constituted as to make available the knowledge and experience of all sections of the community.

In neither case did they refer to economic policy and advice. They commended, however, the model of the Department of Scientific and Industrial Research established in 1915 and drew attention to the Advisory Council which was to be attached to the Department of Commerce and Industry in the Board of Trade.[1]

At the end of 1923 Beveridge wrote an article in *The Nation and Athenaeum* advocating the creation of an economic general staff at the Cabinet level on the lines of the Committee of Imperial Defence.[2] This weekly was edited by Hubert Henderson, and Keynes was chairman of the company which owned it. Beveridge argued that governments were faced with problems in the field of economic science as technical as those in the field of military and naval science. He envisaged a body which would stand above the departments headed by 'a person of high authority in the science of economics, and of corresponding authority in the public service'.

The idea was considered by the Labour Government under Ramsay MacDonald which came into office in January 1924, with Haldane as Lord Chancellor. In July, a Treasury memorandum entitled 'Foresight and Co-ordination in Economic Enquiry' was accepted by the Cabinet. There was to be a Committee of Economic Inquiry which would be able to summon outside economic and statistical experts to advise on particular problems. However, the government fell at the beginning of November 1924 without having brought the Committee into being.

The succeeding Conservative Government under Stanley Baldwin widened the idea by creating, in 1925, a Committee of Civil Research charged with the duty of 'giving connected forethought from a central standpoint to the development of economic, scientific and statistical research in relation to civil policy and administration'. It was intended that the economic side of the work should be linked with the Board of Trade by way of the Chief Economic Adviser. On the analogy of the Committee of Imperial Defence, the only permanent member was the Prime Minister. From the beginning the Committee acquired a strong colonial and scientific bias. Occasionally it tackled an economic issue, e.g. the iron and steel industry, but it had no permanent economic staff nor did it draw much on professional economic advice. In any case much of that field was being covered by the Balfour Committee on Industry and Trade. After his initial enthusiasm Baldwin lost interest and the Committee had lost importance by 1927.

Nevertheless outside Whitehall the idea of an economic general staff continued to be actively discussed. The idea was developed, for example, at some length in the Liberal Yellow Book on 'Britain's Industrial Future' published in 1928, Keynes and Henderson being members of the group which produced it. The problem of unemployment and possible solutions were a major issue at the May 1929 General Election from which the Labour Party emerged with the largest number of seats. The party had pledged to set up a National Economic Committee. It would create permanent machinery through which 'scientific knowledge and technical skill may be mobilised for improving the organisation of industry, increasing economic efficiency, and raising the standard of life throughout the whole community'. Towards the end of 1929 MacDonald had a series of luncheon meetings with economists, businessmen and trade unionists. From these meetings emerged the Economic Advisory Council which was announced early in 1930.[3] The Council was:

(i) To advise His Majesty's Government in economic matters.
(ii) To make continuous study of developments in trade and industry and in the use of national and imperial resources, of the effect of legislation and fiscal policy at home and abroad, and of all aspects of national, imperial and international economy with a bearing on the prosperity of the country.

Like the Committee it replaced, the Council was a standing body reporting to the Cabinet. It included four ministers in addition to the Prime Minister, the Chancellor of the Exchequer, Lord Privy Seal (in effect

Minister for Unemployment), the President of the Board of Trade, and the Minister of Agriculture and Fisheries. There were to be added persons chosen 'in virtue of their special knowledge and experience of industry and economics'.

In February 1930 fifteen names were announced as being members in the last category—seven industrialists, two trade union officials (Bevin and Citrine), two scientists, three economists (Keynes, G. D. H. Cole and Josiah Stamp) and an economic historian (R. H. Tawney). Hubert Henderson was persuaded to become joint secretary and Colin Clark, an Oxford pupil of Cole's, became a member of a very small secretariat.

The Council, however, made a somewhat wider use of professional economists on its committees. The Committee of Economists set up in the summer of 1930, with Keynes in the Chair, included Professors A. C. Pigou and Lionel Robbins as well as Henderson and Stamp. Richard (now Lord) Kahn acted as joint secretary of this committee.

The Council ceased to meet in January 1932 and the Committee of Economists was dissolved during 1931. Two standing committees, however, remained in being: on Economic Information until July 1939 and on Scientific Research until January 1938.

Two other points need to be made about the period prior to 1939. First, the absence of formal appointment did not mean that ministers were without economic advice. For a long time it had been usual, for example, for the Chancellor of the Exchequer and the President of the Board of Trade to draw on the advice of trusted friends and acquaintances in the City and industry. They may even have consulted academic economists. Senior civil servants also had their contacts in the world outside Whitehall. But such advisers were not given any formal status in the department.

Second, between 1919 and 1946 there existed a post of Chief Economic Adviser.[4] The first holder was Sir Hubert Llewellyn Smith.[5] As Permanent Secretary of the Board of Trade since January 1907 he found the increasing pressure of work as the department expanded left him 'less and less leisure to take a comprehensive survey of economic developments and tendencies as a whole'. The new officer stood somewhat outside the general stream of current departmental business. His duties were mainly as British member of the Economic Committee of the League of Nations and he was a delegate to Conferences on economic subjects convened by the League. He was also United Kingdom representative on the Imperial Shipping Committee and the Imperial Economic Conference. Llewellyn Smith retired in 1927 to be succeeded by Sir Sydney Chapman, who was followed in 1932 by Sir Frederick Leith-Ross, Deputy Controller of Finance in the Treasury, who remained domiciled in that department. Leith-Ross had the title of Chief Economic Adviser to HMG, whereas Llewellyn Smith and Chapman were Chief Economic Advisers to the Board of Trade. At the outbreak of war Leith-Ross became Director General of the Ministry of Economic Warfare.

The original conception of the office was wider than it developed in practice. When the Board of Trade was reorganised in 1917–18 a new General Economic Department was set up. In essence it was an Intelligence Department but Llewellyn Smith envisaged the temporary recruitment of economics graduates, i.e. of 'inners and outers'. Lord Waverley has recorded that he was consulted on a proposal to establish an Economic General Staff in the Board of Trade.[6] The new section did not however last very long and appears to have been disbanded about 1922, the office of Chief

Economic Adviser remaining as the sole embodiment of the idea that government could benefit from the services of the economist. Little has yet been published about the work and influence of the holders of this post.

II

The war of 1939–45 led to a considerable recruitment of economists from the universities. The majority were used to administer the various forms of government control, for example Gaitskell, Kahn, Reddaway and Tout in the Board of Trade; and Hall, Jewkes and Plant in the Ministries of Supply and of Aircraft Production. A small number were used as 'advisers': for example, Henderson, Keynes and Robertson in the Treasury; Meade, Robbins and Austin Robinson in the Economic Section; and Harrod and MacDougall with Professor Lindemann (adviser to Mr Churchill). They were all appointed as temporaries, usually on leave from their university posts. Very quickly after the war was over they left the government service. Only a few remained, e.g. Sir Harry Campion as head of the Central Statistical Office.

The major institutional innovation was the creation of an Economic Section in the offices of the War Cabinet. It came about in this way. The threat of war had created serious concern about the government's preparedness not only militarily but in respect of finance and production. An influential group of MPs recommended, as part of a scheme of Economic Defence, the formation of an Economic General Staff. This resulted in what became known as the Stamp Survey—a trio of Sir Josiah (Lord) Stamp, Henry Clay and Hubert Henderson. A few months later, war having broken out, Stamp was given the title of Adviser on Economic Co-operation and became chairman of an official Interdepartmental Committee on Economic Policy, a development conceived as merely an extension of the Survey.

In November 1939 a small number of economists and statisticians were recruited as temporaries to operate a Central Economic Information Service working under the direction of Stamp's Committee. In view of the wide scope of their work, they were placed, at Sir Horace Wilson's suggestion, in the Cabinet Office, not in the Treasury. In January 1941 the Stamp Committee was finally dissolved. The Central Economic Information Service was divided into two parts—a Central Statistical Office and an Economic Section. The former was to be a common service unit charged with the task of providing reliable and standardised statistics. The latter became advisers to the Lord President who had emerged as the senior co-ordinating minister on the home front.[7]

Sir John Anderson (later Lord Waverley) told his ministerial colleagues in November 1943 that the Economic Section consisted of a Director and eight assistants recruited from academic life. Each member was allocated a particular sphere of work not covered exclusively by the activities of a single administrative department, e.g. manpower, shipping, national income and expenditure. It was their duty to be acquainted with departmental activities in their allotted spheres and to keep *au courant de* any scientific developments in that sphere. They kept in touch with departmental activities partly by a variety of informal contacts, partly by membership of relevant interdepartmental committees at the official level. The Section by then was circulating a 'Quarterly Survey of the General Economic Position' but its main work consisted of reports or minutes to the Lord President on current issues or on items appearing on the agenda of the Lord President's Committee.[8]

Arising out of the discussions which led to the publication in May 1944 of the White Paper on Employment Policy, the Coalition Government expressed their intention 'to establish on a permanent basis a small central staff qualified to measure and analyse economic trends and submit appreciations of them to the Ministers concerned'. The White Paper took the view that, particularly during the crucial early years of the scheme for maintaining full employment, the responsibilities of this central staff would be very heavy, for many of the decisions required to carry out employment policy would depend on quick and accurate diagnosis.[9]

The post-war arrangements for government economic advice had already been discussed shortly before that by a Ministerial Machinery of Government Committee under the chairmanship of Sir John Anderson. Two broad questions predominated: (a) Should economists be placed in a central position or be scattered throughout the departments? (b) How should they be recruited?

Robbins envisaged the continuation of an Economic Section based in the Cabinet Offices attached to a minister or group of ministers. He wanted to maintain this central section, not disperse its members among the departments. He thought that economists so recruited, at the centre, would rise above a narrow departmental view and give more independent advice to ministers. In contrast, Sir Donald Fergusson (then Permanent Secretary, the Ministry of Agriculture and Fisheries) was against such a central body arguing that it would cut across the responsibility of ministers for their departments. He secured some support from Hubert Henderson. Keynes whilst believing that more economists should be located within the individual departments supported Robbins' plea for a central economic staff. As for the location of this Economic Section, Robbins believed that the Cabinet would prove most suitable. Keynes did not disagree but also thought the Treasury would need to have a smaller group of economists for its own purposes. As regards recruitment there was a general belief in the appointment of 'inners and outers' on secondment from the universities for periods of three to five years.[10]

At the end of the war, therefore, the Economic Section remained in being in the Cabinet Office. The Director (Lionel, later Lord, Robbins) returned to his Chair at the London School of Economics, and most of the other members returned to the universities. James Meade, however, stayed on as Robbins' successor until 1947, to be succeeded by Robert Hall who had joined the section from the Ministry of Supply in 1946. The section remained small, usually around eight or so economists and a Director. The senior members had all taught economics in a university from which they were usually on leave of absence.

During June–July 1947, following the fuel crisis and a general dissatisfaction with the Government's economic planning (the phrase used in preference to economic policy), an Economic Planning Board, a high-level advisory body, under the chairmanship of Sir Edwin (later Lord) Plowden as Chief Planning Officer, was established to work directly for the Lord President (Herbert Morrison) who was also the minister advised by the Economic Section. The Board was also given the help of a Central Economic Planning Staff, of interdepartmental officials. However, on 29 September the Prime Minister announced that Sir Stafford Cripps was to take up a new post of Minister of Economic Affairs. The Planning Board and Staff would work under him and he was also given the assistance of the Economic Section.

The experiment of having both a Minister for Economic Affairs and a Minister for 'Finance', i.e. the Chancellor of the Exchequer, was never seriously put to the test. On 13 November Dalton resigned as Chancellor to be succeeded by Cripps who took with him his functions in respect of economic affairs. And so the Chief Planning Officer and the Economic Planning Staff, but not the Economic Section, became part of the Treasury. In the autumn of 1953, however, the Chief Planning Officer resigned and the Economic Planning Staff and the Economic Section came within the purview of a newly-appointed Deputy to the Permanent Secretary to the Treasury, who also became Chairman of the Economic Planning Board. The head of the Economic Section became Economic Adviser to HMG and in fact adviser to the Chancellor of the Exchequer.[11]

The transfer of the Economic Section from the Cabinet Office to the Treasury was no doubt inevitable, for no non-departmental minister could stand for long against the prestige and authority of a Chancellor of the Exchequer backed by the ability and expertise of the Treasury. The change, however, left ministers with no alternative professional economic advice to that proffered by the Chancellor. In passing, however, it should be noted that when Churchill became Prime Minister again in November 1951 he appointed Lord Cherwell to his former post of Paymaster–General, who in turn brought back Donald MacDougall who recruited several academic economists. Cherwell returned to his Oxford Chair two years later and his economists also returned to academic life. Even so, for about two years, the Prime Minister had the advantage of advice on economic affairs other than from the Treasury.

Early in 1962 the Economic Planning Board was abolished and a National Economic Development Council established. This advisory body was to be a meeting ground for ministers and representatives of both sides of industry. Its staff was composed of career civil servants, recruits from industry and academic economists.

Notwithstanding these various developments, hardly any professional economists were employed in the other departments, if we exclude the specialist group of agricultural economists in the Ministry of Agriculture and Fisheries. At the beginning of 1964 the Economist group of the Civil Service totalled about twenty-one of whom all but four were in the Treasury. In 1960 David Henderson could claim that the Board of Trade and the Ministries of Labour and Transport had neither an economic section nor an economist.[12] Booth and Coats[13] say the reason was the unwillingness of the Treasury to offer the level of salaries and conditions of employment to attract academic economists at a time when the universities were restocking and the demand for professional economists far exceeded the supply. Moreover, many of the likeliest recruits had already spent four or five years in the service and were very happy to be back once again in academic life. But had ministers and the Civil Service been very keen on recruiting professional economists they would have found ways of achieving this, as is evidenced by the experience of the National Economic Development Council and the developments after October 1964.

The coming into office of Harold Wilson's Administration in October 1964 led to a big increase in the number of professional economists employed in the Civil Service. Part of the expansion was due to the creation of a Department of Economic Affairs (under

George Brown), but the departments concerned with the Environment, Transport, Trade and Industry, and Overseas Development also became big users. By 1966 the number had grown to 70 or 80; by 1967 to around 120, and by 1973 to 262. In April 1980 the Government Economic Service, covering all departments, was around 380. In addition the Bank of England employed over 100 economists.

The increase led to a change in the character of the recruitment and tenure. Almost all the economists now employed in the Government Economic Service are recruited straight after graduate work or at a comparatively early age, e.g. after a short period of university teaching. Moreover they are conceived as a career staff, not 'inners and outers'. They have been assimilated to the normal pattern of the Civil Service.

The situation is thus extremely different from that prior to 1939 or even to that of the 1950s. Then, Whitehall contained only a handful of professional economists either part-time, e.g. in the case of the Economic Advisory Council, or full-time, e.g. in the Economic Section, in which case they were temporary recruits from the universities. Now they are a very numerous career service. What do the changes imply for the role and status of the economist in Whitehall?

III

It does not mean that economists are twenty or so times more influential in the formulation of government policy than they were in the 1940s. The great bulk of the Government Economic Service are not engaged on advising ministers in the sense that the term was used in the early years of the Economic Section. Many are engaged on analytical and statistical work including the appraisal of trends in particular sectors of the economy. Very many more are confined to monitoring and maintaining a forecasting model either generally or for a limited part of the economy. Their contributions may ultimately form part of the data or findings on which policy decisions are formulated. But they are required to exercise little or no judgement in their work about what such policy should be.

There has, however, been a significant extension of their influence in the micro field, e.g. transport, housing, and industry and trade. The Green Papers on Monopolies and Mergers Policy of May 1978 and on Restrictive Practices Policy of March 1979 were examples of this influence.

In any discussion of the role of government economists the terms 'economic intelligence' and 'economic information' are far more often used than 'economic advice'. The White Paper on Employment Policy said the economic staff would 'measure and analyse economic trends and submit appreciations of them.' In a recent paper on the economist in government, Edward (Lord) Boyle, a former Treasury minister, put economic intelligence and economic forecasting as the first and second functions of a government economist, with policy advice third.[14]

As regards the third function he quoted Cairncross as saying that the economist is 'advising the administrators far more than he is advising the minister'.[15] The advice, Boyle added, 'must be clear, begging no questions, and capable of withstanding a process of filtering. Otherwise administrators will turn his advice into a part of what they themselves want to say. Even when an economic adviser is closest to his minister, his advice will still be more effective if the views of the Permanent Secretary have been moving in the same direction.'[16]

The increase in numbers has not weakened the role of the administration group as policy advisers to ministers. Indeed so far as decisions involving economics are concerned the group is probably better placed now than at any time in the present century. For one thing, the big increase in the teaching of economics in universities has been reflected in the recruitment of administrative trainees. The number of senior administrators with economics degrees rose from 11 in 1956 to 157 in 1965. A study of the higher civil service showed that in 1971 over a quarter of the Permanent, Deputy and Under–Secretaries had degrees in social studies (excluding law).[17]

Moreover, the basic concepts of economics and the tools of the economics trade are now taught to all administrative recruits. My impression of the senior Civil Service of 1940–45 was that they were handicapped in their approach to economic problems not by a lack of a highly technical training in great depth but more often by a failure to think in the way that economists had been trained to think, e.g. as to the relationship between different elements in the economic system, marginal analysis, opportunity costs etc. A major feature of the Treasury Centre for Administrative Studies opened in October 1963 was the emphasis on economics and statistical and mathematical techniques. More than half the time of the 20-week course was spent on the concepts of micro- and macro-economics followed by the study of a series of current economic problems, e.g. the balance of payments, pricing and investment policy in the public sector, and the problems of developing countries.[18]

The teaching of economics to non-economists is now a function of the Civil Service College. There is a general Introductory Course of 20 days with shorter, 5-day courses on international trade, industry and social policy. These are in addition to the 8-week course for Administration trainees. As a result the Administration group are no longer the ignoramuses about economic theory that they were in the inter-war years.

At the same time as the administrative civil servant has been making himself familiar with the language and concepts of economics the prestige of the professional economist has declined. It has, of course, long been part of the Whitehall tradition that experts should be on tap, not on top; that most ministerial decisions need to be based on a series of considerations: political, administrative, financial, and technical. But at one time there were some who thought that only professional economists were competent to advise on the solution of economic problems. Few would make such a claim now. Many, including many economists, would not merely doubt that, but would even doubt whether the knowledge and expertise of the professional economist could provide the major ingredient in the decision-making process. There are two main reasons for this scepticism: first, quite eminent economists are capable of differing widely on the advice they proffer, e.g. on whether or not imports should be limited or the value of the pound sterling lowered. Second, there is an increasing realisation that it is politics rather than economic theory that must in many cases dictate the kind of immediate action to be taken, e.g. as regards the course of wages and prices.

Professional economists may disagree among themselves for several reasons. Though the body of economic theory has grown out of all recognition during the past 30–40 years and is now presented with all the refinement and precision that mathematics can apparently provide there are still areas of doubt and disagreement. For some years it looked as though Keynes had united all economists in their attitude to some of the central issues of the economic system but that consensus has now disappeared. A combination of inflation and mass unemployment has put the economic policy advisers in some disarray.

Even where there is agreement on theory there may be serious differences of opinion on the quantitative aspects of a problem. The area of possible disagreement should be less now that the government collects, processes and publishes a much greater volume of statistics and information. Even so, there must inevitably be some gaps or areas of uncertainty where judgement or guesswork replaces knowledge. And it is not unknown for the beauty and precision of a mathematical formula to disguise the poor quality of the data to which the formula has to be applied.

It is also quite easy for professional economists to disagree as to the reactions of particular interests and the public generally to the policies they may advocate. For example, how will other countries react to the imposition of quotas on their exports to Britain or what kind of incomes policy will receive general trade union support. Finally, professional economists may differ about the goals of economic policy. Some, for example, may believe that greater equality, whether of incomes within a country or between developed and third world countries, should be the target. Their beliefs may be justified by reference to economic theory but more likely they are in-built attitudes or derived from a broad view of human values. It is these general beliefs which find their way into the programmes of the political parties.

Some economists may, in pursuit of general beliefs, advocate or support measures which bring them very much into the party political arena, e.g. the nationalisation of industry or the State direction of investment. They may or may not support their views by profound economic analysis: they may indeed appear to be somewhat split personalities, professional economists in some matters, party politicians in others.

What do these differing views of economists mean in terms of their employment by ministers?

The point was raised by Hubert Henderson in the discussions in 1943–44. He then said,

> Under ordinary peace conditions the issues on which economists differ may be leading issues of party controversy: so that the Ministers to be advised are in effect committed on the one side or the other by virtue of their political position. Under such conditions, the last thing Ministers want is ostensibly expert advice. What they want are (1) arguments on their side of the case which may be useful as munitions in debate, and (2) advice as to the best course to pursue in a detailed application of a predetermined line of policy. For both these functions, economists doubtless have their uses, though neither represents very satisfactory or happy scope for exercise of their higher faculties.

As a result he thought it might be necessary to change the personnel of the Economic Section *en bloc* with each change of ministry.[19] Neither Keynes, nor Robbins nor the other commentators appeared to have considered that would be necessary or likely. They must have envisaged a core of economic theory and advice not greatly affected by personal or party political views.

Henderson was no doubt drawing on his experience as joint secretary of the Economic Advisory Council. Indeed his appointment had led to some criticism in the Labour Party, for Henderson was closely linked with Liberal Party policy. The Independent Labour Party weekly *New Leader* argued that a socialist economist should have been appointed.[20] The views of professional economists, e.g. in the Committee of Economists, were by no means unanimous in their diagnosis of present problems and the possible remedies. Keynes was the Chairman, the other members being Henderson, Pigou, Robbins and Stamp, with Richard (now Lord) Kahn as joint secretary. The final report of 24 October 1930 contained an agreed diagnosis, and a majority endorsed some of Keynes's policy proposals. But the agreement was based on an 'uneasy compromise between points of view that remained deeply divided on fundamental questions of analysis and terminology.... Political and other value-judgments were inevitably brought into play.'[21] There were, for example, major differences of opinion on the wisdom of a revenue tariff and on wage policy. The Cabinet Committee of ministers to whom the report was referred found it a disappointing document. 'There was a lack of unanimity in its conclusions and ... it contained no practical propositions to which immediate effect could be given.'[22] It is little wonder that the Economic Advisory Council was not consulted during the financial and economic crisis of 1931.

IV

Notwithstanding the political content of economic policy, there was no evidence of political influence in the staffing of the Economic Section. It contained people of widely differing political persuasions. Lionel Robbins, for example, differed from James Meade on the extent to which the State should interfere in economic affairs. Robert Hall, who became head of the Economic Section in 1947, and his senior colleagues, advised both Labour and Conservative governments. Cairncross, who succeeded him in 1961 under the Tories, had earlier served as Economic Adviser under two Labour Presidents of the Board of Trade (Sir Stafford Cripps and Harold Wilson).

The first public evidence of a different attitude came in October 1964 with the arrival of Harold Wilson at No. 10 Downing Street. The new government announced three new economic appointments at the centre, excluding the new Department of Economic Affairs. They were Thomas Balogh, Nicholas Kaldor and Robert Neild. Balogh was given the title of Adviser on Economic Affairs to the Cabinet and Kaldor was described as Special Adviser to the Chancellor of the Exchequer on the Social and Economic Aspects of Taxation Policy. All three could be regarded as political appointments. Balogh had been a member of the Economic and Financial Committee of the Labour Party for 20 years and both Kaldor and Neild were publicly associated with the Labour Party and, in particular, with Mr Callaghan. Sam Brittan gave them the title of 'The Irregulars.'

The roles given to Balogh and Kaldor were sufficiently special, and their position in the governmental machine sufficiently distinctive, not to raise many problems. But Neild's appointment in the Treasury raised the issue of his relationship with the Economic Section and its head. It was not just a question of title. Balogh's appointment, and the establishment of a Department of Economic Affairs with Donald MacDougall as its Director General, made it very difficult, if not impossible, to retain the title of Economic Adviser to Her Majesty's Government for the head of the Economic Section. But that title had only been conferred in 1953: for the ten or so years before that his title had simply been Director of the Economic Section.

By 1964 the Economic Section was a settled part of the Treasury, and under its head (Alec Cairncross) provided economic advice to the Chancellor of the Exchequer and the Treasury generally. The appointment of Neild to the Treasury therefore raised the question of whether he was to replace or to supplement Cairncross. The former was assumed in some quarters, e.g. the *Guardian*. Cairncross, it was suggested, was being shunted into the post of Economic Ambassador in Washington left vacant by the appointment of Eric Roll as Permanent Secretary to the Ministry of Economic Affairs. Cairncross was by then an established civil servant and therefore in no danger of being left without a post, indeed he had the offer of several attractive posts outside the Service. Had he left, Neild would almost certainly have become head of the Economic Section.

Cairncross, however, thought that a major point of principle was involved. He stressed that Neild's appointment would be widely interpreted as making that post for the first time a political appointment.[23] It would carry the implication that Neild would have to leave the post when the Labour Party lost office, indeed he would probably wish to do so. It must be remembered that Wilson had obtained only the barest of bare majorities and therefore another election was likely to be needed in the near future. In the event of a Conservative victory the new Prime Minister would be tempted to follow this precedent and appoint a professional economist of his political persuasion. The effect would be to throw serious doubt on whether economists could pursue a professional career in the Civil Service without regard to the political complexion of the government. It would probably make it difficult in future to recruit academic economists of standing.

After a good deal of top-level discussion Neild was

given the title of Economic Adviser to the Treasury, the Economic Section remaining under Cairncross. Shortly afterwards a Government Economic Service was created covering all departments with Cairncross as its head. The Economic Section became part of the Service but continued to be based in the Treasury and therefore available to advise the department.

When Neild resigned in 1967 to become Director of the Stockholm Institute of International Peace Research the political character of his post was continued by the appointment of Michael Posner who, at that time, had a reputation as a left-wing economist. Balogh and Kaldor ceased to hold full-time appointments on their return to Oxford and Cambridge in 1967–8 (and Posner in 1969). Cairncross resigned from the Government Economic Service in January 1969 on becoming Master of St Peter's College, Oxford. He was replaced by Sir Donald MacDougall who had been Economic Director of the National Economic Development Council (1962–4) and then Director General of the now abolished Department of Economic Affairs. In addition to being head of the Government Economic Service MacDougall also acquired the title of Chief Economic Adviser to the Treasury.

When the Labour Party, still under Harold Wilson's leadership, next came into power in March 1974, they introduced a general system of 'special' or 'political' advisers. (His predecessor, Edward Heath, had made a few similar appointments: for example, Douglas Hurd and Brian Reading.) These advisers were appointed from outside the Civil Service on a temporary basis, for the duration of a particular Administration. They were either connected with the Labour Party or were known to be supporters of the party and its policies. Several (the so-called 'chocolate soldiers') had already been working for the politicians concerned, having up to then been financed by the Rowntree Trust. For a short while there were as many as 40 such appointments, but 25 to 30 was more usual. In November 1974 there were 26 special advisers, 15 full- and 11 part-time. Six were employed at No. 10, four in the Department of Health and Social Security, and three each in Industry and Prices and Consumer Protection. In March 1976 the number had risen to 28. Only a handful of these special advisers were economists. Kaldor returned to the Treasury as Lord Kaldor for a while as a Special Adviser to the Chancellor of the Exchequer. Michael Posner became a Special Adviser in the Ministry of Energy but then was appointed Deputy Chief Economic Adviser in 1975, returning to Cambridge after a year. The head of the Prime Minister's Policy Unit was a Lecturer in Politics but with a working knowledge of economics and he had one professional economist on his small staff.

These advisers were quite openly party-political appointments. As the Armitage Committee said in 1978: 'Although on some occasions the nature of the advice given [by the special adviser] may not be different from that of a career civil servant a fundamental difference remains between [them]'. The special adviser 'is required to exercise his or her political judgment in advising a Minister to make a certain decision. The career civil servant, *per contra*, would refrain from doing so since his position is one of political neutrality.' For that reason the Committee were of the opinion that the rules applicable to career civil servants should not be applied to special advisers.[24]

The extent and character of the appointments resulted in a good deal of criticism from the Opposition and constitutional purists. But before long the general feeling in Whitehall was that within limits it was a useful, indeed a desirable, development. The expenditure Committee of the House of Commons reported in 1977 that there was merit in the system of ministers bringing in a limited number of special advisers, for only with the assistance of such advisers could ministers 'maintain a level of political control over an increasing Civil Service'. Sir John Hunt, then Secretary of the Cabinet, told the Committee that he believed in the system and thought that on the whole it had worked well.[25] This view is apparently shared by the Conservatives, if not to the same extent. For they have put a limit of one special adviser per minister out of public funds as against two with the Labour Government. A minister may with the Prime Minister's permission have more than one but usually providing the other is paid from non-public sources. By the end of 1980, ministers had some 16 to 20 special advisers.

V

This narrative of events poses the question of the character of at least the senior economic posts in the Civil Service. We have noted that the system of 'inners and outers' has now been almost entirely replaced by the Government Economic Service becoming an established career.

The head of the Government Economic Service would, however, appear to be a semi-political appointment, i.e. it need not be filled by appointment from within the Service. Of the eight heads of the Economic Section between 1946 and 1964, and of the Government Economic Service between 1964 and 1980, all had spent part of their working career as university teachers and all but one had already had a period in the Section or as a government economist. Yet only one could have been said to have progressed to the office by the normal

Civil Service process. Taking the period since 1964, Cairncross was succeeded in 1969 by Sir Donald MacDougall who had held various senior economic appointments in Whitehall mainly on leave from his Oxford teaching post. He in turn was succeeded in 1973 by Sir Kenneth Berrill who had been brought into the Treasury from Cambridge in 1965 and had then been Chairman of the University Grants Committee. He moved in the following year to be Director General of the Central Policy Review Staff and was succeeded by Sir Bryan Hopkin. This was an interesting appointment. Hopkin had had a great deal of experience in Whitehall and indeed had been Deputy Chief Economic Adviser during 1970–2. He had then left to become Professor of Economics at Cardiff. Though he reached the age of 60 in December 1974 he was appointed Chief Economic Adviser and Head of the Government Economic Service in December 1974 holding the post on leave of absence from his Chair. Sir Fred Atkinson who succeeded him in May 1977 had spent most of his working life as a government economist, mostly in the Treasury but also in several other departments. He reached the normal retiring age in December 1979. The filling of the vacancy therefore fell to the Conservative Government which had come into office at the May election. They appointed Professor Terry Burns of the London Business School. The LBS had been a critic of the Keynesian policies of the Treasury and Burns had a reputation as a monetarist, which coincided with the outlook of Mrs Thatcher, Sir Geoffrey Howe and other leading Conservatives. Burns had not previously held an appointment in Whitehall.

The appointment of Professor Alan Walters in January 1981 as Economic Adviser to the Prime Minister, like the appointment of Lord Balogh in October 1964, did not raise any new issue of principle so far as the Government Economic Service was concerned. Prime Ministers clearly feel the need to have a source of economic advice other than the Treasury.

It is interesting, though idle, to speculate what would have happened had Atkinson's sixtieth birthday been either earlier, say March 1979, or a year or two later, i.e. December 1980 or 1981. In the former case the appointment would have fallen to Mr Callaghan and Mr Healey who would have been most unlikely to have chosen Professor Burns. In the latter case the Conservatives would either have had to delay the appointment of somebody such as Burns, or have brought him in as a Special Adviser or moved Atkinson to some other post and appointed their own Chief Economic Adviser.

That one can write in these terms shows that, however much the Government Economic Service may have been assimilated to the normal Civil Service career pattern, the appointment and tenure of the head of it has not yet been assimilated to those of the Permanent Secretary of the Treasury. The short period in office of Chief Economic Advisers must both reflect and facilitate this attitude. It is understood that Professor Burns was appointed for four years.

The earlier proposal of the recruitment of 'inners and outers' did not, of course, arise out of a desire to have regard to the political views of the party in power. It reflected a belief that the intellectual environment of the universities was likely to produce livelier, more original, and better economic theorists than would a long period in Whitehall. It also offered any government a much wider choice of talent than if they had been confined to that already employed in the Service. Again an adviser who has an academic post waiting for him can afford to take a more independent view than one whose promotion prospects may be affected by his speaking out of turn or against the prevailing opinion in Whitehall. Finally, in the words of a former Permanent Secretary to the Treasury (Sir Warren Fisher), 'The Public would not be impressed by an "Economic General Staff" which resolved itself into a mere addition of half a dozen more "bureaucrats".'[26] An economist who has spent most of his working life anonymously in the Civil Service is unlikely to have the glamour or be as well known to politicians and the press as one who has been able to express his views freely in the learned journals and in the mass media.

Circumstances rather than a change of policy have probably dictated the present situation. It has never been easy for a university teacher to obtain more than two years leave of absence, though three years has sometimes been possible. Accepting a government appointment for a longer period usually means giving up the academic job which in turn means taking a risk or assuming a Civil Service career. Notwithstanding Civil Service salaries being now so much higher than academic salaries, the number of university teachers interested in such secondment is limited, for only a minority are seriously interested in tackling current problems. Even more limited is the number who would be likely to prove first class at the job. Again what was a feasible exercise when there were only ten or so senior posts becomes impossible when there are a hundred or so. In any case a great deal of the work now performed by the Government Economic Service would not attract a university teacher.

Once, however, the concept of a career service becomes well accepted it will be more difficult to return to a system of 'inners and outers'. For a career service implies a ladder of promotion in which years of unexciting work at the lower levels are ultimately rewarded by the plums at the top. Yet most 'inners and outers' are only attracted by the plums. The very able young graduates who enter the Government Economic Service rather than university teaching are unlikely to accept as readily as did Keynes and Robbins that a university environment produces the best economists. They will try and keep themselves fresh by the occasional year away from Whitehall.

So far as ministers and the politically-minded are concerned the concept of a career service raises the question of the character of the advice likely to be given. It implies that the work of economists in Whitehall is similar to that of the career administrator: both are capable of being equally loyal to and equally capable of serving and advising Labour Ministers one year and Conservative Ministers the next. Though 'inners and outers' were not chosen on party grounds they were likely to include economists of different views and, in most cases, changed fairly frequently.

Earlier we noted the belief in many quarters, and particularly in the Labour Party, that the work of the career Civil Service for ministers needed to be supplemented by advisers politically motivated and reliable. Many Labour Party supporters appear to hold the view that neutral advisers, in the Civil Service sense of the term, hide supporters of the present system and are unlikely to be enthusiastic about or sympathetic to the policies advocated by the Left.

This belief may become more widespread with the decline in support for Butskellism, which according to Sam Brittan was 'an interesting mixture of planning and freedom based on the economic teaching of Lord Keynes'.[27] In writing the *General Theory*, Keynes aimed 'to bring to an issue the deep divergences of opinion between fellow economists which had for the time being almost destroyed the practical influence of economic theory, and will until they are resolved continue to do so'.[28] He succeeded in achieving a consensus for some forty years. In recent years, however, doubts have increasingly come to be expressed about the validity of Keynes's teaching as a basis for public economic policy. Thus a marked divergence of views has opened up both between and within the political parties.

The treatment of the Government Economic Service as a permanent career service would appear to carry one or more of several implications. First, that as suggested earlier the great bulk of the Service is engaged on work of a statistical, mathematical, econometric nature in which personal or political opinions have no part. Second, that even at the higher levels of the Service there is sufficient agreement on the core of economic theory to make it very difficult for a government economist to allow his thoughts and advice to be diverted from it by party or personal values. He is most unlikely, for example, to accept the view that the consumption of a commodity will rise if its price is doubled, even though it may have been embodied in a unanimous resolution at a recent party conference. In that respect a well-trained, honest economist is little different from a well-trained, honest engineer or physicist. Third, it may be that Hubert Henderson was wrong when he said 'the general run of economists are not very well endowed with the marvellous chameleon-like adaptability of the capable civil servant'.[29] That assumes, of course, that the Treasury mandarins, for example, are chameleon-like, changing colour immediately on contact with a new-coloured Cabinet. Perhaps a much wider range of political adaptability is allowed within the strict confines of agreed economic theory than Henderson envisaged.

Some light on the matter may be obtained from the views expressed at the end of 1973[30] by a number of former members of the President's Council of Economic Advisers when posed with the question: How political must the Council be? There is, of course, a very important difference between the CEA and the Government Economic Service in that members of the latter express their views in private, except when called before a Select Committee, whereas the former are also called upon to express their views in public. It was this 'external' function which aroused most concern at the discussion, but only their internal functions are relevant here.

The then Chairman of the Council (Herbert Stein) suggested nine commandments for the conduct of Council members and these received general support. He laid it down that the CEA should present to the President the best economic information and analysis that it could. He went on

> The honest, objective, options paper is the noblest work of the Council.... The President must be given a fair account of the pros and cons of all the eligible choices. [The council] must be able to distinguish between the strength of its own convictions and the probability of truth.... In choosing its position the council should give particular weight to those long-run, indirect and general consequences of policy which are likely to be underestimated by others who have special interests or who are not economists.... For good economics to be overridden by good politics may sometimes have to be accepted. But for good economics to be overridden by bad politics is a tragedy which should be resisted as far as possible. A council member ... should be prepared to give advice about the operation of the policy that exists, even if it is not his preferred policy and even if he is at the same time urging its revision.

> To think that this cannot be constructively done and that a person can work well only in a world made in his own image is childish ... especially ... for economists, whose whole stock in trade is how to make the best of a given situation.

All this could be summed up, he said, in the word 'honesty'. This was quite different from 'credibility'. The former meant telling the truth, the latter meant saying what the listener expected you to say.

Henry Wallich (a member of the Eisenhower Council, 1959–61) agreed that the adviser should owe the President full candour but if he spoke his mind quite freely and perhaps took extreme positions he might be written off as unrealistic. He could therefore take a view intermediate between his own and the President's. The truthfulness of an adviser could be tested by examining the degree of conflict he will tolerate between his own views and the policies actually pursued by the Administration. He also stressed the need for honesty. Eisenhower had told his Council that what he wanted was their objective, impartial appraisal of economic policies and programmes as professional economists, leaving politics to the politicians.

The views expressed were not very different than those recently expressed by Lord Boyle. What did matter enormously, he said, was that 'government economists should be scrupulous in telling the truth and presenting the news as they see it, and that Ministers should accept this. Our modern democracy doesn't always wish to know the truth, and even good administrators will sometimes be tempted to say "I can't tell the Minister this". But specialists owe it to their training always to put rigour and honesty first.' He did not think there was any real difficulty in asking economists with Labour sympathies to advise Conservative governments and vice versa.[31] What neither Herbert Stein nor Edward Boyle seem prepared to accept is that honesty, however rigidly practised, does not rule out wide differences of opinion about theories, facts and solutions.

Maynard Keynes was a political economist in the old-fashioned use of the term. His views on policy were derived partly from his analysis and theory of the economic system and partly from his views of the kind of political and social system in which he thought people should live. Had he remained eternally youthful, it is interesting to speculate on who would have appointed him as their Chief Economic Adviser during the past twenty years.

NOTES

1. *Report of Committee on Machinery of Government 1918* (Cd. 9230) pp. 6–7, 11–12.
2. S. Howson and D. Winch, *The Economic Advisory Council 1930–1939* (Cambridge: Cambridge University Press, 1977) pp. 10–11. See also Anthea Bennett, 'Advising the Cabinet—the Committee of Civil Research, and the Economic Advisory Council', *Public Administration* (Spring 1978) pp. 51–71.
3. S. Howson and D. Winch, op. cit., pp. 17–29.
4. D. N. Chester and F. M. G. Willson, *The Organization of British Central Government 1914–1956* (London: George Allen & Unwin, 1957) pp. 294–6.
5. Sir Hubert Llewellyn Smith, *The Board of Trade* (London: Putnam, 1928) pp. 239–241.
6. Sir John Anderson, *The Organization of Economic Studies in Relation to Problems of Government*, Stamp Memorial Lecture (1947).
7. Chester and Willson, op. cit., pp. 324–5. See also D. N. Chester, 'The Central Machinery for Economic Policy', in *Lessons of the British War Economy* (Cambridge: Cambridge University Press, 1951).
8. Anderson, op. cit., pp. 15–16. See also L. Robbins, *Autobiography of an Economist* (London: Macmillan, 1971) chapter 8.
9. Cmd. 6527 (1944) p. 26.
10. A. Booth and A. W. Coats, 'Some Wartime Observations on the Role of the Economist in Government', *Oxford Economic Papers*, vol. 32 (1980) pp. 177–99; also J. M. Lee, 'Reviewing the Machinery of Government 1942–1952', unpublished report (1977) p. 79.
11. Chester and Willson, op. cit., pp. 327–30.
12. P. D. Henderson, 'The Use of Economists in British Administration', *Oxford*

Economic Papers, vol. 13, pp. 5–26.
13. A. E. Booth and A. W. Coats, 'The Market for Economists in Britain, 1945–75', *Economic Journal*, vol. 88 (1978) pp. 436–54.
14. J. K. Bowers (ed.), *Inflation, Development and Integration: Essays in Honour of A. J. Brown* (Leeds: University of Leeds Press, 1979) pp. 10–12. See also Sir Alec Cairncross, 'The Work of an Economic Adviser', *Public Administration*, vol. 46 (1968) pp. 1–11.
15. Sir Alec Cairncross, 'Economists in Government', *Lloyds Bank Review* (January 1970) p. 8.
16. Op. cit., p. 12.
17. Peta Sheriff, *Career Patterns in the Higher Civil Service* (London: HMSO, 1976) p. 52.
18. C. D. E. Keeling, 'The Treasury Centre for Administrative Studies', *Public Administration*, vol. 43 (1965) pp. 191–8.
19. Quoted by Booth and Coats, 'Some Wartime Observations on the Role of the Economist in Government,' op. cit., p. 187.
20. Howson and Winch, op. cit., p. 25.
21. Ibid., pp. 50–1.
22. Ibid., p. 78.
23. Neild had, however, been a member of the Economic Section during 1951–6 when a Conservative government was in power.
24. *Committee on Political Activities of Civil Servants*, Cmnd. 7057, pp. 29–40.
25. *Eleventh Report 1976–7*, pp. lxv–lxvi.
26. Quoted by Howson and Winch, op. cit., p. 22.
27. *The Treasury under the Tories 1951–1964* (Harmondsworth: Penguin, 1964) p. 162.
28. Quoted by Howson and Winch, op. cit., p. 72.
29. Quoted by Booth and Coats, 'Some Wartime Observations on the Role of the Economist in Government', op. cit., p. 187.
30. *Challenge* (March–April 1974) pp. 28–42.
31. Bowers (ed.), op. cit., pp. 13–14.

DISCUSSION

Official Discussant

Professor A. W. Coats: In responding to Sir Norman's admirably lucid and balanced account of a long, complex, and in certain respects still controversial story, I propose to concentrate on a few general issues rather than points of detail. Having interviewed some of the *dramatis personae* encountered in his paper and enjoyed privileged access to a small proportion of the vast store of unpublished documents bearing on the war-time and post-war activities of economists in British government,[1] I am only too aware of the gaps and deficiencies of our knowledge of the subject.

Apart from his concluding reference to the President's Council of Economic Advisers in the United States, Chester has, quite legitimately, dealt exclusively with developments in Whitehall. However, it is worth noting that the remarkable post-1939 growth in the employment of professional economists in government is not simply a national, but rather a global phenomenon, about which we have little systematic knowledge.[2] Moreover, even a casual acquaintance with conditions elsewhere immediately raises the question why, given the general acknowledgement of the economists' valuable contribution to British war-time government, the number of official posts reserved for recognised professionals of the species remained so small in Whitehall between 1945 and the mid-1960s.

In accounting for this situation, which appears to be unique among advanced industrial countries, Chester mentions such relevant factors as: the war-time irregulars' desire to return to academic life at the end of hostilities; the preference for 'inners and outers' on limited secondment; and the comparatively unfavourable salaries and career prospects for established Civil Service economists at a time when there was a buoyant demand for their services elsewhere. More important still is his recognition that at the beginning of the 1960s 'had Ministers and the Civil Service been very keen on recruiting professional economists they would have found ways of achieving this'. Why, one may ask, was this desire so conspicuously lacking in the first post-war decade and a half?

The explanation is to be sought in a combination of chance circumstances (e.g. the influence of personalities) and deep-rooted administrative practices and cultural attitudes that were, on the whole, accepted both by the economists themselves and by their prospective employers. In retrospect, this reluctance to break with established ideas and traditions seems more surprising under the Labour government of 1945–51 than under the subsequent Conservative administrations. Apart from the genuine early post-war desire to reform or if necessary replace outmoded economic, social, and political institutions, an ostensibly socialist government might have been expected to favour a more positively interventionist and technocratic style of administration in which economists and other professionals would be assigned a prominent and influential place.[3] By contrast the Conservatives, with their ideological opposition to planning and large-scale government, and their suspicion (recalled by some ex-ministers) that most economists were either socialists, or inclined in that direction, might have been expected to keep their numbers and role at a minimum—which was, indeed, more or less the situation in the 1950s. However thereafter, as Chester has noted, the Tory government's renewed enthusiasm for economic planning led to the creation of 'Neddy' and from that time until the advent of the Wilson administration in October 1964, there was positive pressure, both within Whitehall and beyond, in favour of the employment of more economists and other professionals in and around government. No wonder, perhaps, that our national history is sometimes puzzling to foreign observers!

In personnel terms, the deeply entrenched Civil Service preference for 'generalists' over 'specialists' meant that there would have been powerful internal opposition to any proposal to create a significant number of new high-level economist posts within the prestigious Administrative Class, whose functions were officially described as 'advisory'. As Chester has remarked, few of the war-time economists' tasks were exclusively advisory in any strict sense of the term, and most of the dramatic post-1964 growth in the number of professional economists in Whitehall has been in positions that are only indirectly linked to high-level policy-making. Nevertheless it is appropriate to interpret the term 'advisory' broadly, for much policy-making is initiated and formulated in the middle and upper-middle ranks of the bureaucracy, and once policy decisions have been taken they must be implemented and monitored by staff who are not themselves full-time advisers. Within the ranks of economists in government the growth of numbers has, of course, been accompanied by an increasing hierarchy, specialisation and division of labour—a phenomenon familiar to students of bureaucracy—and this has been a direct consequence of war-time and post-war changes in the character and objectives of British government.

With respect to economists, the distinctive feature of

Whitehall is that the war-time members of the Economic Section had enjoyed parity of esteem with administrators, and that relationship was not questioned after the war. Curiously enough, in 1947 a Statistician Class was created with status and conditions of service parallel to administrators (albeit with far fewer opportunities for promotion into the higher echelons), despite the fact that most statisticians regarded themselves as technical specialists and even wished to avoid involvement in advising on policy. A move to create a comparable Economist Class in 1950–51 proved abortive, partly because the numbers involved were too small, but also because of the desire to preserve the elite status of the Cabinet Office economists and to differentiate them clearly from the economic specialists employed in the agricultural departments. As it transpired the agricultural economists were denied grading and status comparable to other economists until 1975.[4]

One by-product of the preference for generalists was that when a successful applicant with a first class degree in economics was offered a choice between one of the few economist posts and entry into the normal administrative category he naturally preferred the latter, given the comparative career and promotion prospects. As a result there was a gradual dissemination of economic knowledge through the upper Civil Service ranks, and this may have had beneficial effects when governments adopted more actively interventionist economic policies in the 1960s and 1970s. However, it would be a mistake to regard all administrators with economics qualifications as professional economists. Many of them performed no economic functions, in any strict sense of the term, and quickly lost touch with the subject once they entered Whitehall, more especially as economics was becoming more sophisticated both in theoretical and quantitative terms. On the other hand, economics is not so esoteric a subject that it cannot be grasped, even mastered effectively for policy purposes, by non-professionals; and as Chester has noted, with the aid of the CAS in the 1960s some of the leading civil servants brushed up their knowledge and enhanced their existing capacity to learn by doing or 'sitting by Nellie'.

While Civil Service traditions and severe constraints on the supply side (which could only have been fully overcome by positive long-term personnel policies) helped to keep down the numbers of professional economists in post-war Whitehall so, too, did the prevailing conception of economic policy-making and the professional economists' conception of their own functions. In customary British fashion, post-war practice largely followed the successful war-time experiment. The modest recommendations enshrined in the 1944 White Paper on Employment Policy reflected the war-time and post-war professional consensus in favour of Keynesian-type macro-economic policy-making, often referred to as demand management. Up to a point this state of affairs may have been inevitable; but this is not the whole truth. The proposal for departmental economists, mentioned by Chester, was not taken up in most instances other than agriculture, where there was an established pre-war tradition, and where successive governments had accepted special responsibilities. In the Board of Trade, for example, a senior economic advisory post was allowed to lapse when its incumbent went off to an international agency. And the need for high-level economic specialists in the Treasury was apparently met in 1953 when the Economic Section was transferred to that department from the Cabinet Office. One can imagine that some establishment officer breathed a sigh of relief, thinking that this new arrangement would mean an economy of scarce resources.

Matters were, of course, more complicated than that. Undoubtedly supply constraints constituted a large part of the explanation of Britain's unusually heavy, if not unique reliance on 'inners and outers' for its economic expertise. But without denying the advantages of a regular turnover of staff in a high-level economic advisory unit[5] one cannot help feeling that some staunch defenders of the Economic Section's personnel policy have been making a virtue out of necessity, especially when it is appreciated that for some years the Section's permanency was in doubt. Short-service official positions have distinct limitations, as well as strengths, as Harold Wilson's 'irregulars' quickly discovered. It takes time to learn to 'play the machine' effectively, to discover who does what and why, and to adapt to the peculiarities of bureaucratic life. Indeed, it is arguable that some of the war-time and post-war economists may have done this too well.

It may be true, as Lord Robbins has claimed of the war-time Economic Section, that:

> any success we had was due partly to our willingness to become part of the machine and accept its logic rather than pretend to some special status, partly to the willingness with which the best elements among the permanent civil servants were prepared to cooperate. If we had not been prepared to conform to the normal rules and normal routine, or if those who ran the machine had been hostile, the experiment would have failed.[6]

Robbins' remarks probably convey fairly accurately the war-time Economic Section economists' conception of the best way to maximise their effectiveness in dealing with senior administrators. They reflect both his style of leadership and his advice to his subordinates, and the same general outlook seems to have prevailed in the post-war Economic Section. Given their temporary incumbency, most of the post-war members were naturally inclined to accept the Whitehall organisational *status quo* as given. Moreover, although a few remained for a decade or more they tended to regard themselves, and be regarded by permanent civil servants, as academics. Had they too insistently pressed their claims as experts, and emphasised their distinctive professional status, they could easily have been ignored, circumvented, outsmarted or even simply outstayed by established personnel. But while infiltration and assimilation may have been unavoidable, even optimal, short-run strategies, it seems clear that longer-run efforts to increase the numbers and enhance the status of the permanent cadre of Civil Service economists were discouraged. By comparison with their American counterparts British economists of the period had a modest conception of their functions and a weak sense of professional identity. They were, in some respects, closer to the humanist than the social science disciplines. Their training in mathematics and quantitative methods was limited; they neither expected nor utilised much equipment or supporting staff; economic forecasting of the period is often loosely referred to, in retrospect, as 'back-of-the-envelope-stuff'; and given the Whitehall environment, they had positive reasons to avoid being regarded as mere specialists and technicians. There was, moreover, no-one anxious and able to plead their cause effectively.

From the early 1960s, however, well before the advent of the first Wilson administration, the climate of opinion was becoming more favourable to economists both in Whitehall and outside. In addition to the revival of interest in planning noted by Chester, two other developments deserve recognition. One is the

Plowden Committee's Report on *The Control of Public Expenditure* (1961), a by-product of dissatisfaction with the government's and the economy's performance in the late 1950s, which led to an increased concern for the efficient management of resources, including Civil Service personnel. The CAS was one manifestation of the new enthusiasm for personnel training, while the Treasury re-organisation of 1962, primarily designed to improve public expenditure planning, was also intended to integrate the Economic Section economists more closely into Treasury divisions. This was not a dramatic change. But the second, concurrent development was the marked internal growth in the demand for economic expertise. In part this resulted from the rise to positions of influence within the hierarchy of a new generation of officials who, irrespective of whether they themselves were trained in economics, appreciated the value of economic expertise, for example as the result of having worked alongside professional economists either in war-time or after. (And during the same period some of the older generation of officials, who had been unable to communicate effectively with economists, passed from the scene.) Admittedly this growth of perceived demand had little immediate effect on the numbers employed in Whitehall for there were severe supply constraints and the demanders often had unrealistic expectations in specifying the type of individual required. Hence those gloomy establishments officers who feared that each department would want a professional economist unit of its very own were mistaken. Nevertheless Sir Alec Cairncross, the Economic Adviser to HMG, was repeatedly urged to serve as a kind of recruiting agent while endeavouring to retain a nucleus of economists under his aegis; and in this respect the ground was being prepared for the more radical changes after October 1964.

The appointments of Thomas Balogh, Nicholas Kaldor, and Robert Neild certainly constituted a significant landmark in the post-war professionalisation of economics in Whitehall. Unlike some of the organisational changes it was a sudden and, to most people, totally unexpected development, though the possibility of forming ministerial 'Cabinets' of advisers on the Continental model had been under discussion for some time. Although the full story is still unclear, Cairncross was by no means alone in seeing it as a direct threat to the neutral, non-partisan reputation which the existing economic staff had built up, not without difficulty. The new appointments were certainly political. The civil servants recognised the threat of politicisation, and there were strong objections from government economists who suspected that Cairncross was either being passed over or pushed out.

As far as the other 'irregulars' are concerned it is virtually impossible to draw a neat line between those appointed for purely political reasons and those whose professional qualifications alone were sufficient to justify their selection. After all, the new administration offered exciting possibilities, and economists had been eager to enter the public service in war-time or to work for a stimulating new venture like 'Neddy'.

The new appointments were generally welcomed from the Labour Party standpoint, for a variety of reasons. Many of its supporters regarded the senior Civil Service as willing tools of the governing classes, and there had been severe criticism of Conservative economic policies, especially 'stop–go', for which the Treasury 'mandarins' were usually held responsible. Some of the new ministers were determined to demonstrate their unwillingness to become captives of the 'establishment'. Another source of dissatisfaction was the persistence of the preference for 'generalists' over specialists referred to earlier, which was not merely regarded as a product of Oxbridge upper class education but also as wholly inappropriate and irrelevant to the needs of an advanced industrial society.[7]

This is not the place to discuss whether, and if so how far, Labour supporters' criticisms of the Civil Service and suspicions of government economists were warranted. With respect to the latter many critics tended to exaggerate the professional economists' capacity to influence decisions. Furthermore they rarely recognised the useful distinction between political and professional conservatism, which is pertinent to this case.

Whatever their political views, government economists found it difficult to resist assimilation and socialisation into the official machine, even though their stay was usually limited. There was a selective recruitment process which tended to exclude radicals, mavericks, or eccentrics, and this was reinforced by the self-selective tendency whereby some of those well qualified to serve had no desire to do so, either because they preferred academic life or because involvement in policy-making and political processes was distasteful to them. In addition, the potential range of professional opinion was limited by the prevailing Keynesian consensus, and this may have been reinforced by the normal bureaucratic inclination to accept the *status quo* and to resist radical departures, whether they emanate from the right or the left of the political spectrum.

Perhaps, on reflection, there is some consolation in the fact that although the vast majority of government economists are now permanent career civil servants the pressure to conformity, even unanimity, is offset by the profound doctrinal and policy disagreements now extant within the profession!

Are professional economists (whether 'advisers' or otherwise) more 'influential' in Whitehall nowadays than they were in war-time or in the early post-war years? To pose the question in this broad, simplistic form, as many enquirers do, is to invite Chester's ambivalent, inconclusive, but fundamentally inescapable response. While their potential influence has unquestionably increased greatly, so has, in most cases, their professional sense of responsibility and humility. The recent debate about 'monetarism', to choose but one example, has revealed serious differences of opinion and gaps in our knowledge of the operation of a crucial component in the economic system. Hence Sir Norman may even have overstated the extent of prevailing agreement about the 'core of economic theory and advice not greatly affected by personal or party political views'.

NOTES

1. This research has been financed by a grant from the Social Science Research Council.
2. For a preliminary effort to rectify this situation see the essays in A. W. Coats (ed.), *Economists in Government: An International Comparative Study* (Duke University Press, 1981)
3. For a useful survey of post-war attitudes to economic planning by a detached observer see Jacques Leruez, *Economic Planning and Politics in Britain* (London: Martin Robertson, 1975) *passim*.
4. Cf. A. W. Coats, 'The Development of the Agricultural Economics Profession in England', *Journal of Agricultural Economics*, vol. 27 (September 1976) especially pp. 389–91. Agricultural economists were regarded primarily as specialists performing 'technical' rather than 'advisory' functions and, unlike administrators, incapable of working in a variety of departments. Their lower status reflected the prevailing cultural prejudice in favour of 'theoretical', as against 'applied' subjects. Despite the growing Civil Service demand for more economic specialists in the 1960s the agricultural economists were refused membership of the newly created Government Economic Service in 1965.
5. It is interesting to recall Sir Norman's own views on this point: 'I think it is also true that by the end of 1945 the temporaries were beginning to lose their value in this respect [i.e. the possession of a fresh outlook]; their earlier experiences had become heavily overladen with their civil service experience

and they were in danger of losing their different outlook'—cf. 'The Central Machinery for Economic Policy' in D. N. Chester, *Lessons of the British War Economy* (Cambridge: Cambridge University Press, 1951) p. 33.

6. Robbins, *Autobiography of an Economist* (London: Macmillan, 1971) p. 184. Robbins went on to praise the high level administrators and registered his 'strong protest' against the Fulton Committee's draftsmen who depicted them as '"amateurs"—a description whose shallow appropriateness reflects as badly on the understanding of its authors as it does on their capacity to resist the temptation of the slick headline and the cheap appeal'.
7. Some of these views were embodied in a Fabian pamphlet, *The Administrators* (1964), produced by a group of civil servants, economists and Labour supporters. Many of its recommendations were subsequently embodied in the Report of the Fulton Committee on the Civil Service (1968). See also Thomas Balogh 'The Apotheosis of the Dilettante' in Hugh Thomas (ed.), *The Establishment* (London: Blond, 1959), subsequently reprinted in Hugh Thomas (ed.), *Crisis in the Civil Service* (London: Blond, 1968). However, for evidence of deep disagreements among economists with respect to the value of Civil Service reform at this time, see T. W. Hutchison, *Economics and Economic Policy in Britain, 1946–1966: Some Aspects of their Interrelations* (London, 1968) pp. 266–70.

General Discussion

Mr Terence Higgins: I would like to take up one or two of the points which have been made. First of all, if I may refer to a point which Professor Austin Robinson made earlier: I think he said Lord Keynes was still advising us today. I think that may well be so, and in the light of the discovery of the papers from the Macmillan Committee, perhaps the present Treasury Select Committee might like to look at those rather carefully. I always think it's rather a shame that Keynes hasn't actually been in a position to rebut some of the more extreme monetarist arguments which have been made recently.

I would now like to take up one or two points which Sir Norman has just made. I think in the early part of his remarks he said that economists have little scope for exercising judgement; they're not close enough to ministers. I must say that doesn't coincide with my own experience, so I think perhaps it does depend rather on the extent to which the ministers actually want to get into the advice which they are actually being given on any given occasion. I would have thought it certainly the case that as far as economic advice is concerned (however much one may rely initially on econometric models and so on), a very high element of judgement necessarily enters into the form in which that 'printout' is actually presented to ministers.

The question of the Central Policy Review Staff I think is really something quite separate, and I wouldn't see it as strictly competitive. It is a separate operation, very often concerned more with micro-economic matters than with macro-economic matters. But the fundamental point about the 'regulars' and the 'irregulars', I think, is an important one, and it is important that the distinction shouldn't be blurred. One does need to distinguish very clearly if one is in government which of the two one is actually concerned with. But, of course, the suspicion of the regulars does depend a great deal again on the individual minister—for example, to the extent we have any evidence on this, there is a big difference between Dick Crossman's attitude, not only to his regular economists but regulars generally, as against Barbara Castle's—where they both seem to adopt a very different attitude on those particular points.

I wonder if I might finally ask just one question, because it's perhaps a unique opportunity to do so, and that is: as far as Keynes is concerned, I have some difficulty in knowing to what extent he did operate in the way which an economic adviser nowadays, either regular or irregular, operates, and whether he was in the office much of the time—either in the first period or the second period—whether he did join in on the toing and froing of minutes and so on, or whether in fact he only appeared occasionally and produced a fairly massive paper. His actual position, historically, at that time is something which I'm not aware of, and on the other hand there are a number of people in the room who have worked with him.

Sir Norman Chester: May I just take up two points. First of all, supposing you're economic adviser in a department, could you serve Eric Varley equally well as Keith Joseph? That's the sort of problem I'm putting to you. Or, if you were a minister, would you say that a man who successfully advised a predecessor could equally successfully advise me? That's the issue I'm really posing. As for Keynes, I didn't know him as well as many people here. My impression is that he was always about, except when he was in the United States, in Washington, or something like that. He really transcended all levels, he could go to any minister, or any of the top Treasury people, or anybody, because at that time, of course, he was really a remarkable man you might say, and he of course had this great facility of being able to write lucid minutes on almost any subject. But I can assure you that he seemed to be always there and always active, and always in touch with all the people that mattered.

Professor Kaldor: I would just like to clear up some of the historical facts concerning what Sir Norman said, especially since I was very involved in them. I think he accurately described the appointment and functions of both myself and Lord Balogh, but I don't think he was accurate about Robert Neild. I would like to make this clear, because evidently he doesn't know all the facts. Long before the Labour government came into office, there was an agreement among the Shadow Cabinet to divide the Treasury between a long-term Treasury and a short-term Treasury, or a Treasury A and a Treasury B, and to create a Department of Economic Affairs with George Brown at its head. George Brown, knowing this, had to recruit a whole department for himself. He recruited Eric Roll whom he met in Fifth Avenue, New York, and said: 'Eric, you're just the man to be my Permanent Secretary.' Eric Roll was then a chief Treasury man in Washington. He recruited Sir Donald MacDougall, who was in NEDO at the time, and he recruited Robert Neild as his Chief Economist. Now all these people, with the exception perhaps of Eric Roll who was on the permanent established list of civil servants, were temporary civil servants, because everybody who first comes in is a temporary and then becomes established at some stage if he wants to be. But their position has nothing to do with being economists. I mean, Robert Neild obviously was there because of his expert knowledge of economics, but George Brown wanted his advice and he was to be part of George Brown's Ministry. Now after the government came into power, George Brown was very anxious to have Tony Crosland, a very good economist, among his junior ministers (who had in fact been appointed Economic Secretary to the Treasury) and he begged Jim Callaghan to let him have him; whereupon Jim Callaghan said: 'I am willing to do so on one condition, that you give me Robert Neild in return.' And that was an agreement between Callaghan and George Brown. Now Callaghan wanted to replace Alec Cairncross with Robert Neild because he wanted a Chief Economic Adviser of his own choosing, not someone he inherited from the previous government. Alec Cairncross could have had just the same rank, or an even higher rank, as chief Treasury representative in Washington. Alec Cairncross, as it happened, was ill at that time, but he wrote a letter to Harold Wilson (whom he knew very well from the days that he was his adviser in the Board of Trade), and said, in a very convincing way, that he thought he was being turfed out on the grounds that he would not loyally serve the new government. Harold Wilson got terribly annoyed, put his foot down, and told Callaghan he simply can't do that. Now the whole thing was a series of misunderstandings; and politics didn't really come into it. Alec Cairncross wasn't to be moved on the grounds that he was not a Labour Party supporter, and not loyal to Labour, but simply on the grounds that Callaghan preferred Neild as his Chief Economic Adviser. The Treasury was perfectly willing because when a new government comes in a certain amount of reshuffling of posts was considered a perfectly normal thing. It had nothing to do with politics at all. Now when it comes to Tommy Balogh and myself; it is entirely different. We were brought in under the ticket, which Professor Coats mentioned, that it would be a good idea to move towards the French system in which ministers should have a *Chef du Cabinet*, or their own advisers, in order to do their battles with the Civil Service. But to do their battles with the Civil Service does not mean that the ministers thought that the Civil Service was Conservative or antagonistic to their ideas, as indeed is shown by the fact that the Tories later used this device and brought Cockfield into the Treasury in exactly the same position as I was in the previous government. The idea simply was that the Civil Service gradually develops its own set of views and is an autonomous body, which is on the whole naturally conservative. It will always produce five-hundred reasons why X, Y or Z can't be done, and the ministers are in too weak a position, and also too much preoccupied with Parliamentary business and Cabinet business, to be able to effectively counter the sort of negativism that develops in the Civil

Service by its very nature. And it's in order to have someone to help ministers vet such arguments as: Can we really not have a corporation tax? Is it really impossible to have a capital gains tax? Is it really impossible to change the structure of taxation?—that this sort of adviser is useful. I'm talking about myself now. Gaitskell offered me this type of post back in the 1950s. His view was simply this: I know the Treasury; I know the Inland Revenue (and indeed, before him Keynes learned to know the Inland Revenue during the war and often told me how extremely conservative they were) and they say in answer to any innovation that came from the outside, you don't realise the administrative impossibilities and complications involved. For that reason, Gaitskell and Callaghan wanted to have an assistant, so to speak, who could really go through the arguments and vet them and see then whether they stand up or not in a way a minister simply hasn't got the time to do. That is the justification for the *Chef du Cabinet*, and again has nothing to do with being Labour or Conservative. The Civil Service are totally loyal to whichever government is in power. But they believe that it is in the long-run interest of their minister and the country to preserve continuity and to oppose innovations the effects of which have not really been fully explored (having not been tried out).

Index

Page numbers in *italics* indicate authorship of a paper or participation in discussions.